Change Fatigue Revisited

Change Fatigue Revisited

A New Framework for Leading Change

Richard Dool and Tahsin I. Alam

BUSINESS EXPERT PRESS

Leader in applied, concise business books

First published in 2022 by
Business Expert Press, LLC
222 East 46th Street, New York, NY 10017
www.businessexpertpress.com

ISBN-13: 978-1-63742-249-6 (paperback)
ISBN-13: 978-1-63742-250-2 (e-book)

Business Expert Press Human Resource Management and Organizational Behavior Collection

First edition: 2022

10 9 8 7 6 5 4 3 2 1

Description

Leaders today must be able to embed resiliency into their organizations and to reposition change as a natural process. Being an effective change agent has become a critical leadership competency for 21st century leaders. With these factors in mind, we are proposing a new approach to change in this book (the *C⁶ Change Leadership Framework*) as a means to mitigate "change fatigue" and to enhance a leader's ability to positively affect change in their organizations.

This book will enable leaders to manage change in a more proactive, tailored, and engaged manner to increase the likelihood of achieving the expected outcomes of the change initiatives.

Keywords

leadership; leadership communication; change management; organizational renewal; resilience; change fatigue; leading change; change agent; change mindset; adaptability; agile leadership

Contents

"*The greatest danger in times of turbulence is not the turbulence—it is to act with yesterday's logic.*"—**Peter Drucker**

"*The rate of change is not going to slow down anytime soon. If anything, competition in most industries will probably speed up even more in the next few decades.*"—**John Kotter**

"*Change is the law of life. And those who look only to the past or present are certain to miss the future.*"—**President John F. Kennedy**

CHAPTER 1

Introduction

The year 2020 was arguably a year like no other. Leaders and organizations faced a series of overlapping crises, any one of which would have presented substantial difficulties in a normal year. Together, they created unprecedented challenges requiring responses not found in the playbooks or crises past. The global pandemic, economic downturn, social unrest, and the deep political divide interweaved to force leaders to confront organizational assumptions, fundamental structures, and underlying systems relied upon in the past. Leaders were forced to implement changes at speed and often without a full appreciation of how deep and wide the tentacles of these crises would extend. And as we have seen since the pandemic began, even the best calculated response could be upended by new changes or could still result in the dissolvement of a business, both small and large.

While 2020 brought a pandemic, for several years prior, leaders were facing a macroenvironment filled with an unprecedented level of active "stressors." The landscape of the 21st century is characterized by increasing complexity, chaos, technological advances, economic shifts, intense competition, hyperchange, a 24/7 "always on" expectation, and a more nomadic workforce (Völpel 2003; Youngman 2020). Add to these tides the overwhelming nature of endless data and information, both real and misleading, the ability to make decisions in the speed required in this century has become more difficult than ever before. We are in an era which Google Director of Engineering, Ray Kurzweil, called the "age of acceleration," where globalization, technology, and financial markets instill a need for newer, better, faster products and services (Friedman 2016, 187). We have regarded organizations as "systems" that change, grow, or move and in which the variables they must navigate are interacting and changing constantly in response to these interactions, which makes it difficult to predict the outcome (Clegg, Kornberger, and Pitsis 2011; Guastello 2013).

Denning (2018) labeled this environment an "unstoppable revolution."

> The revolution is very simple. Today, organizations are connecting everyone and everything, everywhere and all the time. They are becoming capable of delivering instant, intimate, frictionless value on a large scale. They are creating a world in which people, insights and money interact quickly, easily, and cheaply. For some, the revolution is uplifting and beautiful. For others it is dark and threatening.

Organizations and leaders are also under intense scrutiny from a variety of external and internal stakeholders including customers, suppliers, employees, regulators, community activists, and governance officials. There is also systemic impatience in our "instant" environment, driven by unprecedented access and reach fueled by technological advances (e.g., the rise of social media). The age of Amazon has brought about a global expectation of services and goods "immediately." While some businesses have been able to pivot to this expectation, others have not with many facing the end of their time.

The presence of the noted stressors, intense scrutiny, and systemic impatience compels leaders to adjust to meet these conditions. The demands of the organization's stakeholders and market forces create pressure on the management to act. Leaders must launch change initiatives to meet the challenges they must navigate. So how does this change take place? If the playbooks of past are not as handy as they used to be, what will be the playbook of the future?

Many prescriptive change models treat change as linear, one dimensional, simple, and static. We have learned in 2020 that the actual change experience is nonlinear, complex, messy, three dimensional, and dynamic due to the continuous and overlapping stream of environmental demands.

Well intentioned, but poorly positioned and executed change management prescriptive programs may contribute to organizational dysfunction because leaders frame or position change inappropriately. Or, under pressure to deliver results, leaders launch iterations of the change initiatives if the expected results are not experienced quickly enough. On the immediate receiving end of such drastic change is the company itself, its workers, and middle management. The adage "change is the only constant" is often used to accept, justify, or normalize the rapid change, even poorly executed change initiatives. Such rapid change has negative cost associated with it—an environment where disorientation, shifting priorities, and rapid responses can lead to a condition we have labeled as "Change Fatigue™."

In this new reality, organizations have to change *how they change* and match the pace of change in a manner both responsive yet sustainable. They need to increase their organizational agility, increase flexibility, and infuse into the culture a continuous focus that makes change a natural part of the cultural fabric (Kelley 2016). The fatigue that comes from continuous change will both tax the system and confuse the customer base. Imagine a restaurant that changes its menu almost daily in response to different variables—customer tastes, trendy dishes, supply of ingredients. While in some ways this can be viewed as responsive and agile, the toll it takes on staff, waiters, and the confusion caused to customers looking for consistency is a cost to the business that is not always factored into change decisions.

In 2008, IBM conducted a study with global CEOs (Kelley 2016) and found that the following were factors that presented challenges to an organization's ability to embrace change:

- Changing mindsets and attitudes (58 percent)
- Corporate culture (49 percent)
- Underestimating complexity (35 percent)
- Shortage of resources (33 percent)
- Lack of commitment of senior leaders (32 percent)
- Lack of change know-how (20 percent)
- Lack of motivation of employees (16 percent)

What stands out in the prior list is that with the exception of a shortage of resources, the rest are human trait challenges—from human disposition, emotional inclination, behavioral motivation, and skills development.

In 2014, *Forbes* found that "despite the life-or-death stakes, only 50% of executives say their companies adapt well to new technologies or processes, or are well versed in transformation."

The biggest barrier to overcome is conflicting visions among executive leadership or decision makers, cited by 33% of respondents. This is followed by a lack of internal talent to spearhead or execute business change (28%) and resource/budget constraints (25%).

While it might be easy to read the above and surmise that the failure is in leadership, recent studies have shown that leaders themselves are feeling the effects of continuous change. Segal (2021) noted that:

- Nearly 60 percent of leaders reported they feel used up at the end of the workday, which is a strong indicator of burnout.
- Approximately 44 percent of leaders who feel used up at the end of the day expected to change companies in order to advance; 26 percent expected to leave within the next year.
- Only 20 percent of surveyed leaders believed they were effective at leading virtually, a key element in today's changing landscape.

Brower (2020) captures the need to lead change in this environment: "Change is constant and as a result, people, teams and organizations must build their skills in managing change and fostering flexibility."

Given the systemic impatience in many of the organization's stakeholders, the pace of the environment and the advances in technology, leaders must be able to embed resiliency into the organizational culture and to reposition change as a natural organizational process. It is true that "change is the only constant" will lead to some level of fatigue. But what happens if we take that as a given but prepare organizations to lead within the context of continuous change? If your restaurant must change its menu frequently to keep up with diners' tastes and preferences, how can the owners of the restaurant "retrofit" these changes so as not to cause undue fatigue to everyone involved? With these factors and our high-speed future in front of us, we are proposing a new approach to change in this text (the *C⁶ Change Leadership Framework*), as a means to mitigate "change fatigue."

CHAPTER 2

Context

The Speed of Now

Turbulence is occurring at a blistering pace, leaving many businesses unprepared and vulnerable to the chaos it brings.
—Kotler and Caslione (2009)

The world is changing all around us at an increasing rate and does not appear to be slowing down. The 2020/21 pandemic has added to the pace and complexity of change. That said, change has been increasing in pace for more than 50 years. Kelley (2016) noted that in the last 50 years the average lifespan of a S&P 500 company has dropped from 61 years to 18 years. It took the automobile 90 years to reach 90 percent of U.S. households but only 20 years for the mobile phone to attain the same level of utilization.

Garelli (2016) noted a study finding from McKinsey:

A recent study by McKinsey found that the average lifespan of companies listed in Standard & Poor's 500 was 61 years in 1958. Today, it is less than 18 years. McKinsey believes that, in 2027, 75% of the companies currently quoted on the S&P 500 will have disappeared.

Garelli goes on to note:

As the life expectancy of companies drops, ours is increasing. Since the beginning of the century, 50% of the children born in advanced economies can expect to leave up to 100 years old. In addition, the retirement age will certainly increase. The new generation, the Millennials, will probably have to work longer and will do a lot of job hopping during their lifetimes.

It will imply more flexibility in the labor market and more mobility for employees. Also, an increasing number of people will work outside the traditional setup of corporate employment.

We are in the throes of an unstable environment, which for now appears will remain the status quo for some time to come. Organizations are struggling to increase business agility—their ability to quickly respond to change, adapt products, services, and processes, and potentially reconfigure themselves to meet customer demands (Hugos 2009; Kotter 2014; Friedman 2016).

This environment has been labeled as one characterized by "VUCA" (*volatility, uncertainty, complexity*, and *ambiguity*), where the rules and norms of the past no longer create results that organizations and their consumers desire. "VUCA" was used by the U.S. Army War College (Stiehm and Townsend 2002) to describe the post–Cold War global environment and has been applied to organizational survival (Bennett and Lemoine 2014).

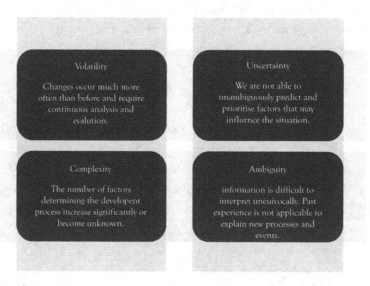

Source: SEEDAdvisory (n.d.)

Simon Sinek (2019) describes this environment as an "infinite game" in his book with the same title. He notes that there are no exact or agreed upon rules, and "winning" is too narrow in perspective. In an infinite game, there is no finish line, but there are infinite time horizons. The primary objective is to keep playing. This speaks to the point that change initiatives should not be treated as events but more appropriately seen as a natural and ongoing daily process. It is a fairly human trait to think that if you solve a problem with an action, that that action will have solved the issue in perpetuity. But as every parent knows, just when you have your newborn in a sleep pattern that you think has stuck, you have to change tactics yet again when only part of that sleep training has stuck. As such, an infinite game, at least for a decade or so.

By its nature, most change is complex, iterative, and politicized (Buchanan 2003).

> In times of ceaseless change, organizations that do not adapt, that do not challenge the status quo, are in danger of irrelevancy— or worse, extinction. Change is accelerating, uniformity is giving way to diversity, and complexity has become every leader's biggest concern. As for businesses, globalization and a rapidly evolving workforce is redefining how we think about competence, creativity, productivity, and the structuring of organizations (Cisco 2011).

Kotler and Casilone, in *Chaotics* (2009), argued for the need to manage differently in what Alan Greenspan referred to as the "age of turbulence." They noted, "Change is the new status quo, leaving managers without firm ground from which to gaze at the onrushing future as markets, technologies, governments, consumers and products undergo constant change with blinding rapidity" (p. 1). Kelley (2016) noted our recent environment was characterized as a "tsunami of change."

Kelley (2016) also noted:

> As far back as 2010, a study by IBM noted that CEOs were worried about the amount of change facing their organizations and not seeing any near-term decrease in change demand. Nearly 50% of the CEOs said they lacked confidence that their organizations had the ability to manage all the change they face. Prosci found in 2013, that 77% of organizations reported they were near the point of change saturation.

The Leaderocity™ (Dool 2021) research project, conducted in 2010 and 2011, explored drivers of the current and foreseen environment including: the emergence of chaotics, systemic impatience, turbulence as the "new normal," the impact of globalization, and the compression of time and space, workforce trends, the digital workplace, the "just in time" workforce, the need to "superstruct," and the culture of connectivity.

Drivers for the Speed of Now

The Emergence of Chaotics (Largely Derived From Kotler and Casilone 2009)

Leaders need to create "chaotics management systems" that allow for "triple planning" (short, mid, and long term), as well as early warning systems, active performance metrics, risk analysis, and information filtration systems. Our traditional strategy life cycles are most likely obsolete or at least under attack. The shelf-life of a strategy is certainly shorter for most organizations and leaders must be more vigilant in seizing opportunities or confronting threats. (Kotler and Caslione 2009). Leaders in the 21st century need to lead three dimensionally across multiple time horizons in what Jeff Immelt, CEO of General Electric, has called a "multispeed" world (Blodget 2015). Think back to the last time a single strategy to change and outcome worked. You may need to go as far back as last decade, or certainly before the current environment of constant information and connectivity. In a presocial media world, you had time to think and react. Now, reactions and feedback are immediate and as such, the change initiative you undertake will need to be able to pivot on multiple reaction speeds.

Systemic Impatience

We are in an era of "now." We are surrounded by "instant" access and response. Examples abound from texting, self-service checkouts, online bill paying, and debit systems. Time is a prized asset and is clearly worth more to an array of both internal and external stakeholders. There is a systemic and societal expectation of "now."

Organizations and leaders as a result are under intense scrutiny from a variety of stakeholders including customers, suppliers, employees, regulators, community activists, and governance officials. Lombardi (1997) dubbed this "the spotlight era" (p. 1). There seems to be a general impatience in both management and its stakeholders and a constant demand for results.

Agility and flexibility have become critical leader and organizational competencies. To become truly agile, an organization must embrace speed as a reality and infuse their operations with speed and dexterity with a strong dose of constant vigilance to changes in the ecosystem. Companies need to be "aerodynamic" (Poscente 2008). It might sometimes feel as if the overall system of our global economy is in a continuous level of stress to deliver goods and services on time. That's not far from the truth. Consider the global supply chain issues amid the effects from the pandemic. The system writ large is already pushed to its limits and ripple effects happen more frequently than ever before.

Turbulence as the New Normal

Capgemini (2005) has noted that managers today must lead in an environment of "permanent volatility." Reilly, Brett, and Stroh (1993) described the environment in which managers must perform as "turbulent," characterized by changes that are, "nontrivial, rapid and discontinuous" (p. 167). While the word turbulence is most often used to describe moments of unease during a flight, even planes have the option of steering away from turbulent air and finding calmer airstreams. Our business and to a degree social reality no longer seems to have an option to veer toward left or right. It is important to note, however, that our human ability to operate in such economic turbulence may not have fully caught up to this adjusted normal. The subsequent fatigue is quickly becoming a palpable reality.

Time and Space Revised

Time and space seem smaller due to the increased reach and access fueled by technology. A 24×7 orientation has become entrenched as stakeholders reach across times and borders to engage on a social or transaction level. Davis noted that "factors of time, space and mass are destroying traditional business solutions. What worked in the industrial world will not work tomorrow." Speed and connectivity will be at the center of new business solutions. Davis (2000) refers to this as the "blur" economy—an economy in continual motion. While in the industrial past companies had proving time to test out new products and services, today's time and space measures—for better and for worse—have created a market that will respond to new offerings at lightning speed. Ideas new today are old and tested by tomorrow, forcing leaders and decision makers to return to the development table on day two.

Interlocking Fragility

Kotler and Caslione (2009) noted that technology and markets are interacting in such a way as to create "interlocking fragility." The actions of players in the market will affect many others which some call the "butterfly effect"—"The interconnected fragility of corporations, markets, banking systems, and nations means that turbulence in one sector creates shocks or changes in another."

Demographics Pentathlon: Multiculturalism Becomes the Norm, The Rise of the "She Economy," Five Generations at Work, Nomadic Workers, and the "Just in Time" Workforce

The U.S. workforce is already one of the most diverse in the world and will become even more so in the coming decades. In fact, by 2050, 30 percent of the U.S. workforce will be Latino. By 2025, 40 percent of U.S. workers may come from a minority background (Meister and Willyerd 2010).

Overall, women made up 46.5 percent of the total U.S. labor force in 2008 according to the Bureau of Labor Statistics (BLS 2018) . The BLS forecasts that women will account for over 50 percent of the increase in total labor force growth by 2030.

> The growing number of women who hold college degrees and have attained influential positions in a variety of organizations is altering the dynamic within formerly male-dominated workplaces.

This process will continue as more women attain leadership positions and societies throughout the world realize the economic and competitive advantages of educating girls and making greater use of their talents as working adults. (Cisco 2011).

We now have five generations at work—employees in their twenties, thirties, forties, fifties, and sixties. We may even see seventies if the aging trends continue. By 2025, the number of Americans over 60 will increase by 70 percent (Institute for the Future 2011). The generation entering work in general is smaller than the one retiring due to declining birth rates. The share of prime-age (25–54 years) workers in the total labor force is projected to decline, from 66 percent in 2010 to 62 percent in 2027, then rise slightly for six years before declining to 61 percent in 2050 (NCBI n.d.).

BLS economist Chuck Pierret has been conducting a study to better assess U.S. worker's job stability over time, interviewing 10,000 individuals, first surveyed in 1979, when group members were between 14 and 22 years old. So far, members of the group have held 10.8 jobs, on average, between ages 18 and 42, using the latest data available (Bureau of Labor Statistics 2018).

"Independent" workers, according to a study by MBO Partners (2011), grew from 16 million to 20 million in 2013, and by 2025 could reach as much as 50 percent of the U.S. workforce as we see the rise of the "gig" economy. "Independent" workers are freelancers, consultants, temporary workers, contractors, or project workers who are deployed on a "just in time" basis as needed. Current trends in the United States support this—Uber, Lyft, TaskRabbit, Upwork, to name a few, are household names that represent some of the biggest companies fueling the "gig economy." While arguments will abound as to how these workers are to be classified from a benefits and tax perspective, ultimately, the demand for this kind of work that lends flexibility to works is only growing.

Informationalization: The Digital Workplace

Davis (2000) noted that today's economy centers around information technology and all businesses must "informationalize" above all else.

Economic value increases faster through the leverage of information assets and more often today companies are making more returns from information-based operations than traditional operations. Consider mega companies such as Facebook, Twitter, and the breadth of the social media infrastructure around the world. While we might be quick to judge these platforms as only socially driven, it is important not to lose sight of the reality that these companies are conducting business with infor-mation and limited to no traditional production of goods and resources. The marketplaces they create certainly facilitate traditional companies; however, they are simultaneously increasing the need for the "informa-tionalization" of companies working with or associated with them. In today's world, it is almost impossible to find a company that has limited to no information readily available to the lay consumer anywhere across the world.

To "SuperStruct"

"New technologies and social media platforms are driving an unprece-dented reorganization of how we produce and create value" (Institute for the Future 2011). To *superstruct* means to create structures that go beyond the basic forms and processes with which we are familiar. It means we have to be willing to collaborate and perform at extreme scales from the micro to the massive. A new generation of organizational concepts and ways of working are emerging. As the pandemic enters well over a year of pushing worker to work from home, a new dialogue has begun about how companies and adapt to a hybrid workplace, a completely remote workplace and returning in full to the office. Such conversations are likely to open, close, or significantly adapt the way we work well into the near and far future. That very conversation has begun to contribute to a reex-amination of how organizational structures take form, both vertically and horizontally, across states and nation states.

B-Team (2015) noted:

Flatter structures not only make sure everybody's voice is heard, they allow companies to make decisions quicker and innovate faster. Flattening an organization isn't just about rearranging an organizational chart. It's about empowering employees to make and participate in decisions and communicate with everyone across the company. It's about empowering employees to make and participate in decisions and communicate with everyone across the company.

One radical way to achieve this is by building a "holacracy." A holacracy is a distributed authority system that uses a set of rules to knit the empowerment of individual employees into the core of an organization.

Unlike conventional top-down or progressive bottom-up approaches, it integrates the benefits of both. Everyone becomes a leader of themselves and their role. In a holacracy, teams organize themselves by using regular task and governance meetings to identify backlogs and conflicts. Rather than being assigned to projects, employees find which projects need their support, based on their agreed job role, not their job title.

Accelerating Interconnections: The Culture of Connectivity, Everyone Is a Networker

Most workers, especially those under 40, are "hyperconnected"—constantly in touch, speaking to each other on multiple platforms, across long distances, and around the globe. Take just your last 24 hours—are you able to confidently say that you have communicated with peers, colleagues, and family on a single communication platform? Further to this, was it only written text, or were there pictures, videos, and phone calls used to complete your full day of interconnectedness? These multiple communication vehicles, unrestricted times of the day, and different formats is blurring the lines between work and home, and leading to a revision of how workers and companies regard the traditional workday. With technology as ever present as it has become, it begs a discussion on if we are truly meant to collaborate in person, over shared social networks, or some combination thereof. Social media networks and platforms show all signs of becoming the primary way workers communicate, connect, and collaborate. We will also see a rise in the use of "corporate social networks" (Meister and Willyerd, 2010). Over a decade ago, social networking platforms were relegated to precisely its namesake—for social purposes. Today, companies not involved in the high-paced corporate social networking platforms stand to lose out on both customers and B2B opportunities. It is likely not a stretch to say that we are unlikely to be a patron to a business today if it does not have an Instagram presence, or not inclined to follow a leader unless they share their thoughts on Twitter. What was once singularly personal is now critical to business.

People almost everywhere are expecting instant access to information and immediate responses to their messages. Human contact is pervasive and conversations never really end. Attention spans seem to be shortening, while tolerance for interruptions is increasing.

Rohit Talwar from FastFuture (Kelley 2016) added these other drivers:

> *"Immersivity"*—By 2025 technology advances may give rise to new immersive live and virtual experiences. Leaders may be able to use this technology to gain insights on change initiatives to test various scenarios and approaches tailored to their organizations.
>
> *Artificial Intelligence*—may be able to be deployed to help the organization learn and adapt strategies and processes and conditions change.

Y Scouts (2018) added in the notion of "new media ecology" as a driver of change:

> New communication tools require new media literacy beyond text. A new ecosystem will take shape around these areas. We are literally developing a new vernacular, a new language for communication between leaders and followers. Between management and staff. At the same time, virtual networks are being integrated more and more seamlessly into our environment and lives, channeling new media into our daily experience without disrupting our desires to connect in person. Social media is beginning to drive social experience as we interact with our virtual and physical worlds interchangeably sharing everything with our networks. Life streaming will likely absorb any last remnant of a life offline, yet we will accept it as it makes us more competitive.

Anderson (B-Team 2015) speaks of "radical transparency." She goes on to say "technology is the campfire around which we tell our stories."

The growth of social networks means people can instantly provide insights, share knowledge and shape opinions. Employees can share thoughts on their employers and campaign against bad practices (B-Team 2015).

This contributes to the "always on" or "instant" expectation that we see in the workplace today. This feeds the systemic impatience that we have discussed as well. It creates a constant tension that frames change as an ever-present force.

The "speed of now" surrounds leaders today and it does not appear that it will slow down anytime soon. Leaders need to navigate this complex environment, addressing the various stressors and effectively lead change at speed. They cannot use time as an excuse and they have to be able to embed flexibility and adaptability into the fabric of the organizations they lead. While in the past it was acceptable for customers to wait for a response from a business, today, not only is a delay not acceptable, a delay is likely to cause a significant loss in online reviews, social networks where conversations about company reputation is omnipresent, and the reality that a single unhappy customer can turn away several customers within hours of a bad experience.

Leaders today need to avoid what Kelley (2016) calls the "deadly change gaps":

- The organization's rate of internal change is slower than that of the rate of external change.
- The speed of innovation is slower than the competition's speed of innovation. This is not just in terms of products or services but also includes process and human capital (talent management and deployment) innovations.
- Resource flexibility, capacity, and capability is less than needed to meet the changes the organization faces.
- The hiring reach and speed is less than adequate to meet the speed of the changes.
- The speed of decision making is slower than needed to meet the demands driven by change.

There is a clear need to balance the demand for speed with intentional, deliberate, and strategic change leadership. Leaders need to reframe change as a natural part of the daily activities of the organization.

Essentially, they need to be able to:

- Create a compelling change vision;
- Communicate it to create broad and deep buy-in among the organization's stakeholders;
- Lead the execution to deliver the expected outcomes; and
- build in resilience and adaptability to address conditions that may emerge.

Sinek (2019) argues for what he calls a "just cause." In what he called the "infinite game" noted earlier, he notes that any leader wishing to lead in this chaotic environment must have a crystal clear "just cause" (change vision). He defines a just cause as a specific vision of a future state that is so appealing that staff are willing to make sacrifices to help advance this vision.

He posits that a "just cause" (change vision) must be:

- For something (affirmative and optimistic)
- Inclusive (open to all those who would like to contribute)
- Service oriented (for the primary benefit of others)
- Resilient (able to endure changes)
- Idealistic (big, bold, and ultimately just over the horizon—aspirational and inspirational)

Larry Fink, CEO of BlackRock (Sinek 2019), made a similar point—the need to develop a "sense of purpose" to frame organizational processes and to create ownership throughout the organization.

Nelson (2011) also made this point about both connecting to the purpose in times of change as well as providing meaningful opportunities to contribute to change initiatives:

Connecting to the head and the heart builds commitment. People are not purely rational. They need to have a rational recognition of the need to change, as well as a deeper emotional connection to believe in what the change is all about. Winning the hearts of the people who will experience the change will make all the difference.

People support what they help create. The movie *Field of Dreams* was close, but not exactly right. It is not "if YOU build it, they will come." But rather, if THEY build it, they will come. People inherently connect with something they help build. Engaging people in the change effort early on will pay out big dividends in the long run.

The need for speed is about getting things done fast and well. The best organizations streamline decisions and processes, empower frontline staff, and break down silos and slow-moving hierarchies (McKinsey 2020). In an era where communication is at high speed, companies have to contend with providing staff with a say in decision making or risk losing them altogether to competitors. While the past, communication up and down the chain took time or were easily filtered or gated out, today there are too many vehicles to communicate feedback across an organizational system. If management actively turns a blind eye to this feedback, they may find themselves a subject of conversation in corporate and private social networks.

McKinsey (2020) suggests that to unleash sustainable speed is a process driven by rethinking ways of working, reimagining organizational structures, and reshaping talent. They highlight examples that include speeding up and driving down decision making, flattening the structure, unleashing nimble and empowered teams, embedding learning as a continuous organizational value, and creating more hybrid work constructs.

They also note the critical need to embed execution excellence.

CEOs who are serious about execution excellence are investing in helping their workforces up their execution game—through targeted programs, realigning incentives, and directing rewards and recognition to teams that execute with speed and excellence.

CHAPTER 3

Change Realities and Dynamics

Sibbet and Wendling (2018) describe change as a "river." Rivers are never the same from one season to the next and often differ a lot from one another. Holes, swirls, big rocks appear and disappear depending on how the water is running. This is a good metaphor for the fluid environment that leaders must navigate to champion and lead change. Part of navigating a river or the chaotic environment (the "speed of now") leaders are experiencing requires a willingness to enter into the unknown. For leaders, entering into the territory of the unknown is essential for change to occur. There are some drivers of change that frame this journey into the unknown.

There are also many myths and anecdotes about change that weave through various change narratives. Brower (2020) offers some of these myths and a bit of "change reality:"

Myth: Everyone gets a vote about the change.
Reality: Give people a voice, not a vote.
Myth: Change management is about selling people on the change.
Reality: Engaging people is much more effective than telling them or selling them.
Myth: If people don't love the new situation, change management has failed.
Reality: No amount of perfect change management can correct for a bad decision, design, or system.
Myth: Good change management involves as many people as possible in as many activities as possible.
Reality: More is better, but too much is too much.

Myth: Change management is fluffy.

Reality: Effective change management influences positive business results.

What Are the Drivers of Change?

As the world continues to diversify into a multitude of industries and a global economy that seems to shift with a high degree of regularity, understanding change and its results requires us to begin at grouping what influences change in the first place. How did Zoom pivot amid the pandemic? Why is it that Amazon's delivery chain was minimally affected during the same time? While both these examples are from two different industries, the ability to pivot from environmental pressures—successfully—tends to have some commonality. Palmer, Dunford, and Akin (2009) identified a set of environmental pressures for change as well as organizational pressures. While it is not easy to apply these factors to an absolute degree, they provide a predictable framework to help us understand the basis of change in organizations and companies at regional, national, and global levels.

The environmental pressures they identified include:

- Fashion pressures (imitating competitors)
- Mandated pressures (legal or regulatory)
- Geopolitical pressures (realignments)
- Hypercompetition pressures
- Reputation or credibility pressures (crises)

These constitute pressures and realities that are largely external to a company but affect both the function and output of an organization at large. For example, the United States quite regularly experiences significant geopolitical pressures as it relates to oil security both domestically and abroad (Krane and Medlock 2018, 562), requiring it to change its approach to importing, exporting, and releasing strategic reserves of oil. General Motors, in response to changing trends in oil and electric vehicles, has declared a doubling down on electric vehicle development, in no small part influenced by competitors' behaviors (LaReau 2021). By that same token, political forces are pushing the U.S. administration to consider significant regulatory changes to gas-powered vehicle sales (Shepardson 2021), which has most companies already preparing for a pivot. And as is the standard in the 21st century amid the almost ubiquitous use of social media as a means for consumers to voice their preferences, customers are voicing their desire for change among the U.S.-based auto companies to take future-proof methods to environmental sustainability (Fortuna 2021). All of this only just within the context of the automotive industry, showing that change can be as much a multiplier effect as it can be a chain effect.

Looking internally organizational pressures include:

- Growth
- Integration
- Identity
- Leadership changes
- Power or political pressures

Leana and Barry (2000) summed up the forces of change as adaptability, cost containment, impatient capital markets, control, and competitive advantage. These pressures and forces of change have become starkly evident during the 2020 global pandemic. Economic growth slowed, companies were forced to integrate both vertically and horizontally for survival much less profit (Nixon 2020), and identity of companies and leadership alike have both flourished and succumbed to the forces of a 24-hour, 360-degree news cycle (Mahoney 2021).

Heerwagen, Kelly, and Kampschroer (2006) note the structure, content, and processes of work have changed. Work is now more cognitively complex. Work is team-based and collaborative. Work is also highly dependent on technology, is time pressured, and becoming more and more mobile. In 2020, we learned that much more can be done for business remotely than ever imagined before, while simultaneously, many businesses—particularly those in the service industry—have shuttered their doors because of a structural inability to change overall (Guzman, Prema, Sood, and Wilkes 2020). Another major change in the way we do business came in the form of an increased need for transparency, internal communication, and how critical both are to the survivability of an organization amid so many change factors (Li, Sun, Tao, and Lee 2021). In fact, these two factors have come together during the pandemic—getting clarity on how mobile or centralized a workforce can be and hearing it clearly and transparently from leadership. Leaders hedging their decisions on the mobile versus centrally located debate are under constant scrutiny by the larger workforce, not only internally but also on external technology platforms that allow different organizational workforces to "compare notes" on work conditions. The days of management allowing for time to pass as the antidote to a confrontation with the workforce are quickly becoming extinct. Transparency is now currency and workforces are demanding that specific payment.

As a result, organizations today are more agile and lean than in the past, more tuned to dynamic competitive requirements and strategy, and continually reorganizing to maintain or gain a competitive advantage. The two key environmental drivers are:

- Increasing pressures on organizations to be more competitive, more agile, more customer focused; in other words, to be a "lean enterprise."
- Communication, reputation, and the use of technology: An organization's social capital and brand in the current age of social media, brand identity, reputation, and activities of key leadership actors.

Team B (2015) captured the drivers of change and some of the associated skills needed in this graphic:

What Does Change Really Look Like?
What Really Changes?

As recently as the first decade of the 21st century, an estimated 46 percent of organizations were undergoing three or more complex change programs at one time (Bareil, Savoie, and Meuier 2007), indicating a need for leaders to accept change as normality (Senior and Swailes 2009), as well as understanding the nature of change. Consider a multitude of

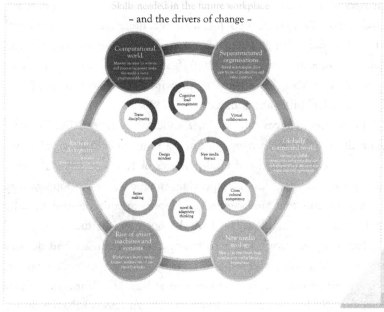

Adapted from Institute for the Future, Future Work Skills 2020, 2011

organizations and companies just in the last two years, inclusive of the pandemic. Companies, both large and small, have shuttered while other companies such as Home Depot have flourished. While the predictability of what would be successful and fail during this time can be up for debate, the unifying reality across all organizational outcomes has been the continuous change experienced and the resilience to stay relevant has contributed to survivability.

Organizational change, or change at its most baseline, has a fleeting definition overall. Hammer and Champy (2009) define this type of change as "the fundamental rethinking and radical redesign of business processes to achieve dramatic improvements in critical, contemporary measures of performance such as cost, quality, service, and speed."

Palmer, Duncan, and Akin (2009) posit the main types of changes tend to be driven by three common organizational or structural changes that include downsizing or rightsizing, technology or systems changes, and realignments (mergers, acquisitions, or divestitures). A fourth could be added with leadership changes (CEO). In a survey in 2006, it was found that 43 percent of companies reported at least two of these types of changes in the prior 12 months (Dool 2006). On the other hand, Aims, Slack, and Hinnings (2004) maintain the literature sees incremental or evolutionary change being interspersed with revolutionary change. Palmer, Duncan, and Akin (2009) further argue that organizations generally face what they labeled as "first order" (incremental change) or "second order" (discontinuous change) (p. 86).

First-order changes can be either anticipatory or reactive. They are generally small-scale changes and often a result of individual initiatives or from the development of local practices or routines. These are often changes as a result of tuning, improving, enhancing, or developing. They are adjustments that are intended to support organizational continuity and order. The year 2020 laid bare the outcomes of such changes, as evidenced by Amazon's ability to increase its marketplace and delivery streams in a seamless and responsive manner to the pandemic economy while other competitors such as Target, Best Buy, J.C. Penny, and J.Crew have filed for bankruptcy (Markowitz 2021). Amazon's behavior during this time can characterized as anticipatory; in seeing the change in the marketplace from the pandemic, Amazon adjusted all parts of its service delivery and warehouse processing to adjust for current and ongoing demand changes. Big box companies such Target and the others previously mentioned who were already under competitive pressure from Amazon, can be seen as having taken a reactive position to the pandemic. As with many businesses globally, these companies to a "wait and see" approach to the pandemic shutdown, perhaps hoping that it would be short-lived. While no one was able to completely predict the extent of the pandemic and its effect on business, Amazon's anticipatory behavior caused them to take immediate action to immediate market changes.

Second-order change is transformational or radical. These types of changes alter the organization and include discontinuous practices such as delayering, outsourcing, disaggregation, down scoping, and changes in internal boundaries (Palmer, Duncan, and Akin 2009). For the most transformational and all-encompassing example of second-order change in this day is the shift of organizations to remote working and the current consideration of continuing that arrangement after the pandemic with a view toward making workplaces more responsive to workers' needs (Thompson 2020). Early in the pandemic, there was significant resistance to a fully mobile workforce, in some cases because of assumptions made by some companies of their inability to conduct business in a remote work environment.

Palmer, Duncan, and Akin (2009) go on to note these second-or-der changes can be characterized as "tectonic" change (large enough to overcome inertia), "punctuated equilibrium" (short bursts of fundamental change), and "robust transformation" (enactment of new capabilities). Further, researchers posit rapid and fast paced change creates a momentum needed to overcome the inertia that build within organizations over time (Aims, Slack, and Hinings 2004). Quattrone and Hopper (2001) argue that change is better defined as drift.

> The idea of drift is preferred to change for several reasons. First, it has no
>
> Connotation that individuals are sufficiently conscious of space and time to transcend the contingent factors facing them. Secondly, there is no assumption that people move from well-defined situations A or B in a linear, predictable, and ordered spatiotemporal framework. Finally, it recognizes contingent factors that actors may be aware of, seek to respond to, but carry them along in unpredictable ways. In organizational terms, drift recognizes the existence of some knowledge of what an organization is, where it is and where it should. However, possession of such knowledge does not transcend actions or outcomes to unknown destinations (427).

Armenakis and Bedeian (1999) identify three areas as common to all efforts to changing an organization; *content, context,* and *process.* *Content* refers to the specifics of the change. Is it an incremental change, made over time or is it a dramatic change that fundamentally changes the organization's way of operating? *Context* refers largely to preexisting forces in the organization's operating environment. *Process* issues are those involving all aspects of communicating the change. *Readiness for change* can be defined as the extent that the organization is prepared, both psychologically and behaviorally, to implement change (Weiner, Amick, and Lee 2008).

Further, Greenwood, and Hinings (1996) propose scope and pace as dimensions of change. Plowman, Baker, Beck, Kulkarni, Solvansky, and Travis (2007) contend the types of change vary along the following dimensions:

- Driver(s) of change: These drivers can be inertia or instability.
- Form of change: The forms could be adaptation or replacement.
- Nature of change: The nature could be emergent or intended.
- Types of feedback and connections: This dimension drives the change and the organizational systems with loose or tight connections (p. 517).

Because of the complexity of change, leading organizational program can be risky (Newman 2000) but can lead to organizational survival in changing environments (Wischnevksy 2004).

Why Do Most Change Initiatives Fail?

Research indicates that change initiatives fail at a high rate (70 percent) (Gill and Whittle 1992; Higgs and Rowland 2000; Miller 2002). The Gartner Group (as cited in Miller 2002) has reported that 28 percent of all major corporate systems investments are abandoned before completion, 46 percent are behind schedule or over budget, and 80 percent are not used as intended or at all within six months of completion. Change initiative failures occur for various reasons including poor strategy decisions, inappropriate choices, poor monitoring and control, lack of resources, leadership impatience, lack of a unifying framework for action, a shift in conditions, the lack of holistic integration, poor execution or poor design, and communications (Garvin 1993). Some change initiatives are launched without any formal structure whatsoever. Failed change initiatives may contribute to employee stress by undermining the employee's capacity to absorb and respond to more change (Sikora, Beaty, and Forward 2004). A classic example of failed change initiatives is the Kodak company. For decades, the industry leader for all things cameras and film, the company displayed a classic example of not recognizing a shift in conditions and making poor strategic decisions. In the face of rising digital adoption of photography, Kodak predetermined that the digital revolution was not going to affect their core business. As a result, Kodak began to see a quick loss of market share followed by a collapse of their market leader position. Despite being a multibillion-dollar company at its height, Kodak filed for bankruptcy in 2012, joining a growing list of companies seeing their downfall due to an inability, or perhaps in unwillingness, to change.

A popular metric is the often-stated 70 percent failure rate for organizational change efforts (Hughes 2011; Senge, Kleiner, Roberts, Ross, Roth, and Smith 1999). This value was mainly established by two *Harvard Business Review* articles: one by Beer, Eisenstat, and Spector (1990), "Why Change Programs Don't Produce Change," and the other by Kotter (1996), "Leading Change: Why Transformation Efforts Fail." Kotter (1996) applies it again in *A Sense of Urgency*, as do Hammer and Champy (2009) in *Reengineering the Corporation: Manifesto for Business Revolution*.

McKinsey (2015) published the results of a survey showing that 40 percent of executives reported their transformation efforts as completely or mostly successful. Many companies claim to be transforming, but when they looked for evidence, successful change efforts seemed to be rare. In their study of S&P 500 and Global 500 firms, they identified only 10 companies that seemed to meet the inclusion criteria for success: new growth, the ability for core repositioning (agility), and financial performance. The companies that stood out as transformational were Amazon, Netflix, Priceline, Apple, Aetna, Adobe, DaVita, Microsoft, Danone, and ThyssenKrupp. Short of conditions of catastrophic failure or tremendous opportunity, organizations are increasingly challenged to make these radical transformational changes. However, identifying and supporting change agents that might take on such tasks is difficult.

There have been many studies that have analyzed the success and failure of various change management programs in various industries and organizations. The problem with these studies is that they have been inconsistent with what constitutes failure and what criteria is employed in the analysis (Hutzschenreuter and Kliendienst 2006).

There are no known measures that can predict the successful implementation of organizational change and it is further complicated when we recognize that change in organizations occurs over time (Carr and Hancock 2006). Implementation can also occur differently in each unit of an organization.

According to Hoag, Ritschard, and Cooper (2002), obstacles to change included poor leadership (such as no vision, a lack of a change policy, a "victim mindset," or saying "this did not succeed before," promoting the status quo, and so forth), internal systems that prevented success, poor communication, a culture that promoted confusion, and the rumor mill (pp. 10–11). An ongoing and current example of such obstacles to change can be found in the United States Postal Service (USPS). A behemoth organization with a confused culture and limited communication on goals and objects, USPS has continued to struggle to stay relevant in the face of electronic communication, market competitors such as UPS and Fedex, and a failure to think beyond a victim mindset. Beyond just its struggles of being a public organization operated with a private mindset, the limited change policies of an organization reliant on "doing things how they have been always done" has resulted in creating a hobbled organization supported by the U.S. government and home to an antiquated work environment.

Another potential cause of change failures is the variable of resistance. In addition, Rosenberg and Mosca (2011) note that individual or personal factors for resisting change came in two dimensions: active and passive.

Resistance to change is often cited by leaders as the reason for change failures Leaders believe workers resist change and as a result do all sorts of things to counter that resistance. But instead of breaking through resistance, leaders may *create* it. People resist being controlled. And so 70 percent of all corporate change efforts "fail," as noted earlier.

To be clear, people do not resist change, they resist *being* changed. Resistance to change is hard to assess, measure, and monitor. Rigid change leadership and management initiatives, with chain-of-command type governance, are often undermined by key stakeholders who resist planned change with skilled use of power, influence, and resources. Management across all levels, not just at leadership, are both key drivers and challengers to change initiatives. Management sometimes is unable to discern the difference between process changes and changes that aim to change people themselves. The former, articulated well, will have a greater chance of success versus the latter which is more likely to fail. For example, most companies during the pandemic changed work processes and conditions to adapt to working from home, provided workers with the resources needed to move with this change, and revising policy to support this rapid and unexpected conversion of classic practices. Companies that kept the focus on changing the method of work tended to see more success during this transition. On the other hand, companies that then followed up such a change with expecting workers at home to be tied to their desks, check in several times a day to prove that they were "at work," and not distracted by personal obligations faced greater resistance from employees than they expected. The difference in these two examples is that the former sought to change work processes versus the latter sought to change employees themselves.

Skilled change management practitioners are able to understand and diagnose resistance in organizational culture, and work within constraints. The more skilled the change agent, the better the chances for success. Change initiatives fail also because the reasons for change have not been made strongly enough and communicated effectively across the organization. Often, it's only the senior leaders who understand the reasons for the changes. Blanchard (n.d.) noted that many change efforts start with all the managers getting together behind closed doors and deciding what should be done. They never think of telling their people what is going to happen and why, let alone canvassing their opinions, ideas, or suggestions because they are the people closest to the front line and who just might be able to see what ultimate impact the change could have on the customer.

There are several reasons for inquiring into resistance because of the various elements that should not be viewed as positive or negative but as a way of managing change (Erwin and Garmann 2010). The outcome of research by Erwin and Garmann (2010) was an identification of cognitive, affective, and behavioral reactions to change. For example, individuals could be predisposed to resist change or have negative thoughts and feelings based on past experiences. These researchers also found managers should:

- Plan for resistance to change. There should be plan for resistance and develop initiatives as part of the change process.
- Provide additional support to workers. This involves identifying workers who are likely to resist change and provide help with defense behaviors.

- Address individual concerns. This can be accomplished by providing opportunities for workers to provide feedback and including them in the decision-making process.
- Provide support and training. In order to build individual and team confidence, provide training and support to successfully implement the change program.
- Communicate. The leader needs to provide clear and frequent communication throughout the change process.
- Ensure understanding of the change. This involves providing details on how the change effort will influence individuals. Also, the leader should explain what is expected.
- Examine policies and behaviors of consistency. It is imperative policies, goals, and management actions are consistent with the change program.
- Develop confidence and trust. This involves gaining buy in to the values of change, openness to constructive criticisms, and demonstrating the needs, benefits, and motivation for the change program.
- Develop efficient management styles. There is a need to encourage collaboration and avoiding the use of power and coercion.
- Develop quality manager–employee relationships. This involves understanding current relationships and development opportunities and making changes as a follow-though with change implementation (pp. 51–52).

In summary, leaders must understand their impact on change success. Leadership mistakes or impatience often leads to change failure. In their rush to change their organizations, leaders end up immersing themselves in an alphabet soup of initiatives (Beer and Nohria 2000). Serial changes due to leadership impatience undermine the ability of the organization to sustain change. Rosenberg and Mosca (2011) conclude that leaders can address the barriers to change by: (1) rooting the concept of change into the organizational culture; (2) hiring workers who accept working in a dynamic environment; and (3) adopting strategies directed to overcome barriers (p. 144).

The Speed of Change

A final aspect of change is the speed at which it is undertaken and attempted. In today's context, it would seem almost unthinkable to effect change in an incremental speed, taking an iterative purposeful approach rather than reacting to the previously mentioned environmental factors that force us to pivot immediately. As observed by Uotila (2017), "in stable and simple environments, incremental changes found to be sufficient to keep pace with the task environment." These kinds of changes are seen most often, somewhat counterintuitively, in invention and innovation. Steam engines to the industrial revolution, jet planes to aviation, and e-commerce to the Internet, are all examples of incremental change in a stable environment where iterative steps were taken to achieve the conveniences and marketplaces we know them to be today (Kishore 2015). The same can be said of high-tech giants such as Amazon, Apple, and Microsoft. While each of these companies make giant leaps in their respective areas, stepping back, we see this change occurring over two to three decades.

This is not to say that transformational or radical change does not have its place. One famous example is that of Netflix, that pivoted rapidly in 2007 from being a DVD-based mail company to an online streaming platform. While the Netflix we know today has made incremental changes to its streaming offerings— original content, documentaries to mini-series, purchasing movies from production houses—its major pivot away from DVDs to online content was planned, executed, and rolled out over the course of just over a year (Venkatraman 2019). Both models of the speed of change have their place in organizational change, yet the outcomes and effects to both employees and consumers can be wide ranging and hard to predict.

CHAPTER 4

Change Models

No Silver Bullets

Leaders facing an unstable environment attempt to deal with change through the conception and implementation of change management programs. Many change management programs or frameworks have been offered by academic theorists and practitioners since the 1970s. These programs often are presented in a form that suggests that change is an event or cycle to be managed (e.g., Kotter, Jick, and Bridges). It could be argued that event- or cycle-focused change management models may not be as effective in a chaotic environment because these models often present change management models as linear, one-dimensional responses. Additionally, the impression could be created in a practitioner that these models have a cycle, and once completed, will effectively manage the change initiative. These models present a series of prescriptive steps that suggest a sequential approach to change management will be effective. However, if change is messy, multilevel, multidimensional, and continuous, it then can be argued that these models may no longer be as appropriate and may contribute to the sources of stress impacting employees. Abrahamson (2004) notes that "most management advice today—whether it is from books or articles, prescribed in courses or by consultants—says that change is good and more change is better" (p. 93). Most change management models are based on three features: (1) "change or perish," (2) "creative destruction," and (3) "no pain, no change." This has led to an environment of "change for change's sake" and has resulted in "initiative overload" (p. 93).

The seeds of the change management theory came with the work of Kurt Lewin (1947) and the notion of resistance to change. Lewin evolved his concept based on the "person as a complex energy field in which all behavior could be conceived of as a change in some state of a field" (Dent and Goldberg 1999, 27). Lewin (1947) wrote, "Change and constancy are relative concepts; group life is never without change, merely differences in the amount and type of change exist" (p. 13). In a section of the paper titled "Constancy and Resistance to Change," Lewin said, "Only by relating the actual degree of constancy to the strength of forces toward or away from the present state of affairs can one speak of degrees of resistance or 'stability' of group life in a given respect" (p. 14). In the same paper, Lewin says that "the practical task of social management, as well as the scientific task of understanding the dynamics of group life, requires insight into the desire for and resistance to, specific change" (p. 14).

Lewin's force-field theory (see Figure 4.1) held that organizations are in dynamic tension between forces pushing for change and forces resistant to change (Trompenaars and Woolliams 2003). Lewin's theories are essentially the foundation for many of the change management models that came years later.

Many change management programs or frameworks have been offered by academic theorists and practitioners since the 1970s but many

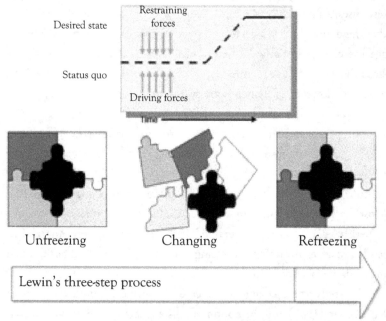

Figure 4.1 Adapted from Lewin's Force-field Theory

emerged in the early 1990s. As noted previously, these programs often are presented in a form that suggests that change is an event or cycle to be managed with a clearly defined beginning and ending. Kotter, Jick, and Bridges offered one of the first "*n-step* guides" (prescribed steps) for change management. Jick's (1991) tactically oriented 10-step model was developed to guide the implementation of major organizational change. Bridges (1991) theorized that "it isn't the changes that do you in, it's the transitions" (p. 3). Kotter (1996) is one of the most prolific and cited change management theorists in the field. Kotter (1996) offered an "eight-step" process for creating major change and addressed the common errors that undermine change initiatives: "establishing a sense of urgency, creating a guiding coalition, developing a vision and strategy, communicating the change vision, empowering broad-based action, generating short-term wins, consolidating gains, and producing more change, and anchoring the new approaches in the culture" (p. 21). While this may sound like a linear approach, it is worth considering that this approach can be used for multiple initiatives in a nonlinear fashion. For example, a multinational company can take this approach to change in different locations at different times based on business needs. A linear approach that is bound to fail for a multinational company would be to use a step-by-step change process for the entire company, all locations, and all departments. Instead, if this company takes a decentralized approach and uses these steps in fashion most adaptable to each business unit, there is a greater chance for success.

Other change management models that emerged include the McKinsey 7-S Framework, the ADKAR model from Prosci, the Satir System, and a practical example—the Change Acceleration Process (CAP) that is used at General Electric.

The McKinsey "7-S Framework" was developed in the 1980s. Essentially this framework analyzes firm's organizational design by looking at seven key internal elements: strategy, structure, systems, shared values, style, staff, and skills, in order to identify if they are effectively aligned and allow organization to achieve its objectives. The model has been widely used by academics and practitioners and remains one of the most popular strategic planning tools. It sought to present an emphasis on human resources (Soft S), rather than the traditional mass production tangibles of capital, infrastructure, and equipment (Hard S), as a key to higher organizational performance. The most common uses of the frame-work are:

- To facilitate organizational change
- To help implement new strategy
- To identify how each area may change in the future
- To facilitate the merger of organizations

The model can help guide organizational change. Managers must act on all Ss in parallel and understand that the factors are interrelated. This interconnectivity creates a dynamic system where one change requires the system to adapt to a new equilibrium. It helps align the processes, systems, people, and values of an organization. Since it analyzes each element and the relationship between them in detail, it ensures that you miss no gaps caused by changed strategies. It has been criticized for focusing on internal elements, while paying no attention to the external elements that may affect organizational performance (creately 2021). This model can be effective in leading change and may be more effective than misinterpreted "*n-step*" models as long as a practitioner does not see the seven steps as linear in nature. The 7-S model has shown particular success with companies or teams that experience a change in scale and size. For example, a company that is either doubling in size due to consumer demand or merging with another company in order to increase market share can benefit from the 7-S model to help align values, strategy, structure, and staff. The 7-S method helps to identify areas of stagnation or lack of equilibrium, thus shining a light on where the decisions for change need to be concentrated. An example is from Coca-Cola. Coca-Cola used this model to create its "6P" Strategic Plan (profit, people, portfolio, partners, planet, productivity). Coca Cola management adjusted its strategy and created it's "6P" strategy based on the McKinsey 7S Framework. The company leadership credits the framework as one of the drivers for why Coca-Cola is still identified as one of the best brands in the world (Jason 2020).

The ADKAR model from Prosci offers a five-stage approach including awareness, desire, knowledge, ability, and reinforcement. It has been widely deployed because of its practical format and "out of the box" orientation. It is highly prescriptive in delivery. That is also one of the criticisms that it is too "cookie cutter" and prescriptive and can be interpreted as a "one approach fits all" model (Smith 2019).

The model is different from many other change management models because it focuses on guiding change at the individual level. In contrast, most change models drive change at the organizational level.

- It focuses on outcomes rather than tasks. Most change management models focus on what needs to be done, but ADKAR focuses on achieving outcomes.
- The model can be used to measure how well the change is progressing. For each step of the model, progress can be measured at the individual level. Any gaps identified can then be rectified.
- The model recognizes that it is ultimately people who facilitate change and not simply processes.
- It provides a clear checklist of things that need to be done to manage change.

The criticism of this model is that it ignores the complexity of change. It may be better suited to smaller change initiatives. Only focusing on the people dimension is not enough to make large-scale change happen (EPM n.d.).

The Satir system developed by Virginia Satir offers a five-stage change model. Her model was based on the notion of transforming from "old status quo" to "new status quo" and included these stages: Late status quo, resistance, chaos, integration, and new status quo. It was based on the idea that organizations that "create a safe environment where people are encouraged to cope increase their capacity for change and are much more able to respond effectively to whatever challenges are thrown their way" (Smith 1997). This model follows the Lewin's (1947) "unfreeze and re-freeze" elements that are inherent in most change models. It does recognize that conditions are more fluid and somewhat chaotic, but again to the practitioner, it could be interpreted as another *n-step model* with its five stages.

The Change Acceleration Process (CAP) that is deployed by General Electric (GE) is another form of a *n-step* approach. It was developed in 1990. The model was created out of research done by GE, which resulted in the realization that even projects with a high degree of technical expertise, without consideration of cultural factors, will likely fail. CAP is a change management strategy and set of tools that ensures effectiveness of change through cultural acceptance.

It offers seven elements: leading change, creating a shared need, shaping a vision, mobilizing commitment, making change last, monitoring progress, and changing systems and structures. Like the others, it has a foundation of Lewin's "unfreeze and re-freeze" bookends and also is similar to Kotter's eight steps.

It is a mixed approach in that it offers a "pilot's checklist" for leading change but also can offer a nonlinear and more flexible approach than the other *n-step* models (Zhang 2014). The skills and tools contained in CAP model guide organizations through the process of accepting change, from creating a shared need, shaping a vision, and mobilizing commitment, to teaching them how to make change last, monitor processes, and change systems and structures to ensure the process can move from its current state to an improved state. CAP has been used at GE in a myriad of ways across all divisions and scope of changes. It was used, as an example, in GE Healthcare Lifesciences on a package consolidation project in the Consumables Division. This resulted in a reduction of the types of packages being deployed by 40 percent and an annual savings of $1.3 million through the carrying of less inventory and also more efficient processing.

N-step change management models may not be as effective in our chaotic environment because these models often are interpreted by practitioners as linear, sequential, one-dimensional responses. These models present a series of prescriptive steps that change leaders may interpret as directed initiatives that must be done in order. These models often treat change as linear, simple, and static, but the actual employee experience is "nonlinear, complex, and dynamic" due to the continuous and overlapping stream of environmental demands (Sikora, Beaty, and Forward 2004, 4).

Yet, many in the greater change community, especially practitioners, still seem to think that following a process, or static change method is the way to go. A few studies in 2015 noted that change often fails for these and other reasons:

- Assuming that change can be managed.
- People are objective and leave their biases at the door.

- Change can be mapped out in steps.
- Change "starts" from a neutral point.
- Change itself is a worthy outcome (IE: look how Agile we are!!) (Little 2015).

We have plenty of reasons for why we think change fails, but can *static methods or standards* solve that problem?

Good change practitioners take relevant components from many processes/methods/frameworks and use the parts that fit their context. The *n-step* models provide an illusion of certainty by giving change managers and executives hope that everything will be okay (Little 2015).

A newer approach to leading change may be needed to meet the messy, fast paced, and somewhat chaotic environment in which leaders must navigate. As Aims, Slack, and Henings (2004) caution, the nature of change at the suborganizational level can consist of reversals and oscillations while the archetypal level consists of incremental changes of one change program after the other. Consequently, the need for change leadership and the understanding of all types and dimensions of change are compounded with the estimate that 70 percent of change programs fail (Maurer 2010).

The point here is that organizations that are successful with change own their own change and build their own method to suit their organization. A more tailored change framework may be more effective in the environment. One that is framed with "meaning," that is, the "why" of the change (the Change Vision). Little (2015) noted the approach needs to be equipped with feedback-driven practices and using an off-the-shelf method puts the focus on executing the method, not building meaning. He also noted that "you cannot plan change to a finite certainty." Finally, Little (2015) stated:

> Building, and evolving, your own approach to change puts you, the change agent, in a servant–leader mindset. If you're adjusting to the system, without being an enabler of dysfunction, you're doing the job well because you're learning how to *dance with the system.*

This was the primary driver for the creation of our new change framework: C^6 framework.

CHAPTER 5

Change Fatigue™ Revisited

My doctoral dissertation research revealed the notion of Change Fatigue™ to a higher degree than expected. The primary purpose of this study was to research the impact of stressors related to continuous change and persistent change management initiatives, hypothesized as *enervative change* (Dool 2006), specifically on the organization's employees' level of job stress and job satisfaction.

Enervative change refers to the negative shift in the level of job satisfaction of an organization's employees as a result of continuous change. The impact of ill-conceived or persistent change initiatives was also considered to determine the impact, if any, on an employee's job satisfaction. It reflects the stage where the energy mobilized by the stress process is beginning to run down and decreased job satisfaction occurs. Enervative change is manifested by a reduction (even slight) in the employee's output, and attitude (cynicism, burnout, resistance), resulting in a decrease in job satisfaction. Think about the last time in any workplace you have experienced change—did it either positively or negatively affect your productivity? Just like economic externalities, enervative change is akin to negative externalities. And as classic economics has taught us, ignoring externalities as less than important will cause long-term problems to the overall system, or in this case, the output of workers in a given workplace.

It was posited that the effects of enervative change are cumulative and lead inevitably to the manifestations indicated above. Our study expected to see a significant inverse relationship between overall job satisfaction and stress (frequency and severity).

This was fairly intuitive and we were not sure it was worthy of a doctoral study. However, up to that point, there had been only eight studies on a similar set of variables and six of them were in the UK.

We decided to test the intersections using two variables: change stress frequency and change severity. We defined change stress frequency as how often each change stressor occurred in the last 12 months. Change stress severity referred to the perceived severity of specific stressor events compared to a standard stressor.

The Subjects and Study Demographics

We were pleased with the response to our study. We had a net participation of 484 subjects out of 1,243 subjects solicited for this research project. Of the participants, 55 percent (n = 614) provided complete survey responses for a net response rate of 49.4 percent. The subject pool was reduced to 484 when subjects who did not work for U.S. companies, subjects from organizations with less than five employees, and subjects with more than 15 direct reports were excluded.

It also reflected a high degree of diversity in gender, age, education, ethnicity, experience, and organizational size.

In our research, 54.8 percent (n = 265) of the respondents were females and 45.2 percent (n = 219) male.

The subjects' ages ranged from 18 to 70 years. The mean age was 40.74 years, the median age was 40.00 years with a standard deviation of 11.03 years.

The subjects were a well-educated group, with 37.6 percent (n = 182) having a bachelor's degree, 21.1 percent (n = 102) with master's degrees, and 3.7 percent (n = 18) with doctoral degrees. The remaining 37.6 percent (n = 182) of the subjects had completed high school as their highest educational level.

These results show that the subjects were predominately white 87.8 percent (n = 425). The other ethnicity categories were represented by African Americans 6.2 percent (n = 30), Asians/Pacific Islanders 3.7 percent (n = 18), Hispanics/Latinos 2.1 percent (n = 10), and American Indians 0.2 percent (n = 1).

The results indicate that the subjects' tenure with their current organization ranged from 1 to 38 years. Every subject had been with their current organization at least 1 year and 82.8 percent (n = 401) between 1 and 12 years. The mean number of years worked was 7.27 years with a standard deviation of 7.72 years.

The subjects were employed by organizations of varied sizes, as measured by the number of employees. The number of employees ranged from 5 to 1,000,000, of which 19.6 percent (n = 95) worked for organizations with less than 50 employees and 48.9 percent (n = 237) for organizations that employed more than 1000.

The Subjects' Experience With Change in Their Current Organizations

The research project's central focus was the impact of persistent change on employee job satisfaction as influenced by increases in employee stress (*enervative change*). The subjects were asked if their organizations had launched any "severe" change initiatives in the last 12 months and whether or not they were personally impacted by these change initiatives ("change frequency"). In their responses, 87.2 percent (n = 422) of the subjects indicated that severe change initiatives had been started in their organizations in the last 12 months, and 71.3 percent (n = 345) indicated that they were personally impacted by the change initiatives (change frequency).

The subjects were also queried on the number of severe change initiatives started in the last 12 months. Of the respondents, 64.5 percent (n = 312) reported that their firms had launched between 1 and 5 severe change initiatives in the last 12 months, 15.5 percent (n = 110) of the organizations had started between 6 and 10 change initiatives, and 7.2 percent (n = 35) reported their organizations had started more than 10 change initiatives.

The subjects were asked to identify the severe change initiatives that their firms had started in the last 12 months. The subjects were asked to select from a list of 12 sample organizational change initiatives (severe) or to select "other" and provide specific examples from their firms. They were asked to check all that apply. The range of "*severe*" change initiatives included macro-level changes such as new systems, changes in operations (leadership, processes, strategy), or reorganizations (mergers or acquisitions) as well as micro-level changes (change frequency; e.g., changes in duties). Reorganizations led the change initiatives started in the last 12 months at 39.7 percent (n = 192), followed by new hardware or software systems at 38.8 percent (n = 188), changes in leadership at 34.1 percent (n = 165), or staff reductions at 32.9 percent (n = 159).

It was alarming when we first saw these results. It defied logic; we did not think any leader or organization would launch more than one or two of these "severe" change initiatives in the same year. We thought we had a serious flaw in our methodology and study data.

When we analyzed the data, we realized that we were actually seeing Change Fatigue™ in action. What was happening is that leaders under pressure or impatient for results were launching iterations to the change initiatives they had launched if positive impacts were not experienced quick enough. In our data, the subjects were listing each iteration as a new change initiative, which led to the high reporting of severe changes in the prior 12 months.

Findings

The underlying assumption of this research was that organizational change increased employee stress and subsequently had a negative impact on employee job satisfaction. Testing of the research hypotheses uncovered several noteworthy findings.

Change was analyzed using a two-by-two matrix to identify change groups. The matrix represents four potential states of an organization (business as usual, reactive, adaptive, and enervative) related to their change profile and levels of job stress (stress frequency and stress severity). Change profile refers to the nature of change in the specific state (quadrant).

> *Business as Usual (I)*—in this mode, the individual and organization go about their work as expected. Stress is of a low frequency, low severity nature and therefore, the individual does not feel an unusual level of stress and adjusts as needed to conditions as they arise. The changes in this quadrant are small in number and are considered part of the normal operations of the firm and therefore do not require abnormal reactions.
>
> *Reactive (II)*—in this mode, the individual and organization must react or immediately respond to a change in conditions (threat or opportunity). Stress is of a low frequency, high severity nature

and must be dealt with in a timely manner. Exogenous shocks (threats or crises) often arise unexpectedly and must be addressed as a priority over normal operations. Stress may increase substantially in reaction to these "shocks." The changes in this quadrant are a result of "reactive responses" and generally require abnormal reactions.

Adaptive (III)—in this mode, the individual or organization continuously adapt to changes in the environment (internally or externally). Stress is of a high frequency, low severity nature. Changes become part of the normal activities of the individual or firm. The ability to adjust to the changing conditions becomes part of the organizational fabric and is seen less as change and more as seamless, natural adaptation. Change becomes continuous and often takes place unintentionally as people go about doing their jobs. This is the ideal state in an environment of continuous change due to constant fluctuations in the macro-environment. In this state, stress is present but it is at a manageable level.

Enervative (IV)—in this mode, the individual experiences a state in which the energy necessary to mobilize the effort to persist, starts to run down and decreased job satisfaction occurs. Stress is of a high frequency, high severity nature. The changes initiated by the firm overwhelms the natural adaptation capabilities of the individual. Employees in this mode display symptoms of increased stress and reduced job satisfaction.

Total job satisfaction demonstrated significant inverse relationships with job stress frequency and job stress severity. The relationship between job satisfaction and job stress frequency was stronger than the relationship between job satisfaction and stress severity. These results indicate that as stress frequency and/or severity increase, job satisfaction decreases.

We compared the change groups (business as usual, adaptive, reactive, and enervative) on multiple variables. The enervative group (high stress severity and high stress intensity) showed the lowest level of job satisfaction, while the business as usual group (low stress frequency and severity) had the highest level of job satisfaction.

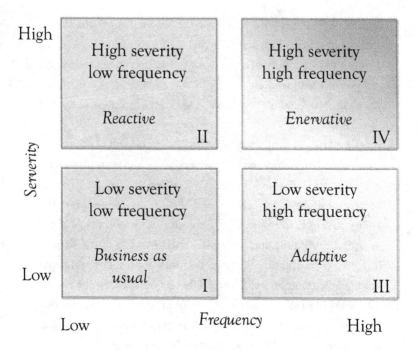

The enervative group had the most number of changes implemented in the past 12 months. Comparing the number of changes organizations started in the last 12 months (1 to 5, 6 to 10, and more than 10) further validated the change matrix model. Subjects reporting 6 to 10 changes indicated more personal impact than subjects with 1 to 5 changes. Subjects with 1 to 5 changes indicated more job satisfaction than subjects with 6 to 10 changes. Subjects with more than 10 changes and subjects with 6 to 10 changes indicated more job stress severity than subjects with 1 to 5 changes. Subjects with more than 10 changes and subjects with 6 to 10 changes indicated more job stress frequency than subjects with 1 to 5 changes.

The research tests validated the underlying assumption that organizational change increases job stress and increased job stress has a negative impact on employee job satisfaction.

Conclusions

This research project has shown that both job stress severity and job stress frequency negatively impact employee job satisfaction. We found that change stress frequency was significantly related to total job satisfaction, the number of change initiatives started, and being personally impacted by the changes. Also, the change group comparisons indicated that subjects who reported more change also reported more personal impact, less job satisfaction, and more stress severity and frequency.

The concept of *enervative change* was sustained by the research results. The enervative group reported the highest levels of change initiatives started in the last 12 months, the highest level of personal impact by the change initiatives and the lowest level of job satisfaction among the change groups.

There was clear evidence that there is a significant inverse relationship between employee total job satisfaction and the individual elements of total job stress (change stress frequency and change stress severity). Surprisingly, the results indicated that change stress frequency had a more negative impact on employee job satisfaction than change stress severity. This is inconsistent with much of the literature on change management, which tends to focus more on the macro change events such as corporate downsizing, mergers and acquisitions, and reorganizations. It was also inconsistent with the sense of the 10 subject matter experts with whom we reviewed the study results. I (Dool) had been a CEO for 10 years when this study was launched and I also had assumed that change severity would have a larger negative impact on employee stress.

We concluded in our study at the time that the presence of *enervative change* in the workplace should not go unaddressed by management. Persistent change initiatives have been shown to increase employee job stress. Increased job stress leads to reduced job satisfaction, which is often manifested in absenteeism, tardiness, and turnover. The costs to the firm of reduced job satisfaction are very high, especially given the increases in competition and the demanding nature of its customers. Given the presence of ineffective change models and the subsequent high failure rate of change initiatives, it is clear that organizations must consider alternative means to managing change.

The literature since our study (2006) indicates that many firms are still launching persistent (serial or overlapping) change initiatives. Clearly, one way to reduce the negative effects of *enervative change* is to reduce the number of change initiatives launched by the organization. If recent history is a guide, this seems unlikely. The systemic impatience between organizational leaders and their stakeholders as well as the volatility in the environment indicates depending on a reduction in change initiatives is not a reasonable position. It would certainly help and should be encouraged but another approach will also need to be pursued.

An alternative to reducing the number of change initiatives is to reframe the notion of "change" and to create a change management framework that encourages a more adaptive organization.

Change management programs seem to be most effective when they are firm-specific. One of the challenges to the traditional change models is that they assume a "one-size-fits-all" approach. This is unrealistic. Change may have many common characteristics, but in practice, change is a situational and a specific experience for employees. Therefore, we offered a new "framework," not a specific model. It is meant as a means to "frame" organizational strategies, processes, and tactics, in order to improve the organization's flexibility, agility, and to reduce the stress related to change.

In our original study, we suggested a new change management framework, the "C^5" framework, be deployed as a means to moderate the stress related to organizational change.

Since the study, we conducted more research and tested our proposed framework in two cases. This experience led us to revisit Change Fatigue™ for this text and to amend our framework to an updated version, the "C^6" framework.

CHAPTER 6

Effective Change Agents

Leading Change, the Agile Leader

There are few things as evident in the study of leadership during the 2020 pandemic than the importance of leadership in managing change. The pre-pandemic world already embraced adaptability in most facets of business and life, but the efficacy of leadership in adapting to change and leading communities through this change has never been more evident. N-step change processes (either dynamic or one of), organizational changes, and reactionary changes, regardless to the pros and cons so far discussed, are all managed and led by management and leaders. The skill sets and characteristics of an effective change agent—discussed later—are just as crucial to change leadership as is the steps taken to effect the change. In today's world, there is an expectation that leaders of organizations, companies, countries, and conglomerates are quick to act, transformative in their action, transparent in their aim and ultimate goals, and openly vulnerable when mistakes are made. In previous decades, slower communication realities allowed some leaders to "hide" when change was either imminent or had been conducted badly. Today, on an almost instantaneous level, leaders are held accountable by customers, middle management, and employees alike. As such, agility has become the most valuable of traits in leadership. How quickly can one pivot? In pivoting, can one communicate the reason for the pivot and articulate to all constituencies how the change will benefit or affect them? Is the CEO's vision and direction embraced by middle management and thereby communicated down the organization to frontline employees? And to what degree is the leader willing to be answerable and available for everything from answering questions to being answerable for failures?

The CEO even in an established business is in a difficult position today, and the CEO responsible for adding change to the system is even harder to find.

Adaptive leaders such as the founder and CEO of Zoom, Eric S. Yuan, have reflected on how adaptability and using change as an opportunity has helped him pivot in a vastly changing marketplace (Nazar 2021). For the company that has arguably been on the spearhead of surviving and thriving in the pandemic, his philosophy has been singular—to communicate well with your teams, be involved in hiring practices, and engendering an environment of risk-taking, all of which is embodied in his attitude of leading by example. These leadership traits can be seen to stretch across other successful CEOs such as Richard Branson of the Virgin Group and Howard Schultz of Starbucks. For all the three leaders, adaptability has been a guiding force in decision making, communication, and strategic direction.

Similarly, Jeff Bezos of Amazon has led with adaptability as a central focus in everything his leadership team and managers do, for taking risks to encouraging employees to think as if they were owners of the company (Sattar 2020). Bezos has engendered a culture of embracing new experiences as often as possible, a leadership trait that permeates the company culture. As we will see in the next section, characteristics such as these result in building an adaptive culture only if the leader is able to communicate values, beliefs, and guiding principles deep into the organization at large, making communication a central part of any adaptive leader's success. As observed by Keating (2021),

> For leaders, adaptability is about having ready access to different ways of thinking, enabling leaders to shift and experiment as things change. Having an elastic cognitive approach allows leaders to use different thinking strategies and mental frameworks. Deepening awareness and perspective help leaders to understand how they think, how their team thinks, and how their customers think.

To fully appreciate adaptive leadership, it is important to also appropriately define adaptability in a business context.

Adaptability is a soft skill that means being able to rapidly learn new skills and behaviors in response to changing circumstances. Employers usually look for adaptability when hiring new staff and the skill is often included in job descriptions because of its importance for growth within a role. Someone demonstrating adaptability in the workplace is flexible and has the ability to respond effectively to their working conditions—even if things don't go as planned. They usually work well on their own *and* with team members. People in leadership positions are often expected to manage unusual situations without explicit instruction. An adaptable leader must be able to solve problems in a fast-paced environment and trust their judgment when making difficult decisions, while still recognizing that what worked before is not necessarily the answer.

In fact, of the variety of leadership characteristics that a leader can possess, it can be argued that adaptability in our current world context is easily the most important facet of a successful leader. While leadership characteristics often bring to mind definition such as confidence, compassion, and communication, an underrated trait is fearlessness and change management, both of which are features of an adaptive leader (Capece 2019). Capece goes on to reflect on how an adaptive leader has an influence on long-term strategic planning. Most often, leaders that are not adaptive are unlikely to create strategic plans that offer flexibility and adaptation to market circumstances in the future. A classic example of this is the lack of adaptive anticipatory planning on the part of Yahoo. As observed by Dwoskin (2016),

> ...the company failed to adapt quickly enough to the two major trends of the consumer Internet: the rise of social networks and the exploding popularity of mobile devices. The latter was perhaps the most brutal for Yahoo. Display ads do not translate well on small screens, and consumers spend much more time on apps than they do surfing the mobile Web. Yet, with the exception of Yahoo Mail, Yahoo's mobile apps never became big hits for iPhone or Android users. Today, despite substantial investments in mobile

products by Yahoo chief executive Marissa Mayer, the company's apps do not rank among the top 50 in Apple's app store in the United States, according to analytics company App Annie. By comparison, Google and Facebook together own eight of the top apps in the United States. In addition, mobile advertising generated just $250 million in revenue for Yahoo in the past quarter. Facebook made $4.5 billion from mobile ads in the last three months of 2015.

Actions, Principles, and Traits of an Adaptive Leader

As with most leadership traits, leading by example and embracing the tenets that a leader preaches is the most effective means of penetrating that style into the greater organization. Leaders who preach innovation yet squelch risk-taking will best create a misunderstanding and at worst create unrealistic expectations for the company bottom line. For example, leaders who preach research and development but do not fund those activities will only be adaptive in talk and not in practice. Further, other than just embracing adaptability on their own, leaders need to impart the same attitude to other managers and leaders throughout the organization.

However, in order to get to this point, leaders themselves need some core tenets to use in order to become innovative and pass on this innovation to their own teams. As observed by Hamel and Tennant (2015),

> ...it makes little sense to hold leaders accountable for innovation if they haven't been trained and coached to encourage innovation within their own teams. For a leader, this means:

- Being adept at using innovation tools.
- Creating frequent opportunities for blue-sky thinking.
- Avoiding premature judgments when evaluating new options.
- Demonstrating an appetite for unconventional ideas.
- Recognizing innovators and celebrating "smart failures."
- Personally mentoring innovation teams.
- Freeing up time and money for innovation.

- Hiring and promoting for creativity.
- Working to eliminate bureaucratic impediments to innovation.
- Understanding and applying the principles of rapid prototyping and low-cost experimentation.

In our experience, most leadership development programs give scant attention to these innovation-enabling attitudes and behaviors. Through selection, training, and feedback, companies must work hard to create a cadre of leaders who are as adept at fostering innovation as they are at running the business.

Hammel and Tennent's aforementioned list provides a good set of actions for an adaptive leader to embody and disseminate throughout the organization. The characteristics, however, of an adaptive leader are decidedly different. While certain characteristics can be developed, other characteristics are sometimes inherent to leaders, especially when they come on board a new to an organization. There is an incredible amount of literature on leadership characteristics in general. Characteristics specifically around adaptability are more specific and pointed.

A frequently referenced body of work on adaptive leadership can be found in *The Practice of Adaptive Leadership: Tools and Tactics for Changing Your Organization and the World* (Heifetz, Linsky, and Grashow 2009). In their work, Heifetz et al. define four foundation principles of effective adaptive leadership, as summarized by Indeed (2021):

So how does a leader actively utilize these traits in a situational or case setting? Heifetz et al. (2009) provide a three-step iterative process involving the following in order:

1. Observe
2. Interpret
3. Intervene

They have found that these steps, practiced appropriately, allows leaders to maintain an adaptive outlook on both micro- and macro-based challenges. Heifetz et al. cautioned that observation can quickly become a subjective matter, with individuals looking at the same

Table 6.1 Adaptive Leadership Attributes

Organizational justice	Organizational justice in adaptive leadership could be described as an open-door policy. It is about keeping open and honest lines of communication with all employees and taking a genuine interest in their questions, concerns, and even criticisms.
Emotional intelligence	Starting from the bottom, emotional intelligence is perhaps the most important characteristic an adaptive leader must possess. Sometimes referred to as emotional quotient ("EQ," for example, as a counterpart to one's "IQ"), emotional intelligence is basically a combination of being both highly self-aware and be aware of others. It is the ability to regulate one's own emotions and also regulate the way one reacts to others' emotions. Leaders with strong emotional intelligence are empathetic, calm, fair, and true team players.
Development	The adaptive leadership model recognizes that organizations must adjust and adapt to stay relevant in a complex and ever-changing marketplace. Additionally, adaptive leaders recognize that developing individuals within the organization is just as important as organizationwide change. Adaptive leaders empower their colleagues and employees to learn and grow through the process of organizational change.
Character	Adaptive leaders demonstrate ethical responsibility and morality. They are transparent in their communication style and hold themselves to the same standards to which they hold their team.

problem in different ways. In order to be successful in observation as an adaptive leader, it is important to be as objective as possible. They encourage a high-level review of what is presented. For example, a ground-level understanding of conflict within a team would involve interviewing and understanding what the challenges are between team members. An observational approach by an adaptive leader instead takes a higher-level point of view—what is going on with the team at large and how are other systems contributing to the current challenges within the team.

Interpreting the situation on the other hand presents a different set of challenges beyond observation. As the word would imply, interpretation requires considering data from a variety of sources, not just the first set of details a leader receives. Similar to considering different viewpoints on a particular subject, an adaptive leader is open and agile enough to consider different assessments of a situation at hand even if the considerations are seemingly contradictory. It is the practice of seeing these different viewpoints and using them regularly to make decisions that leads to adaptability. As noted by Heifetz et al. (2009),

> ...if you are skilled at adaptive leadership, you might find yourself actively holding more than one interpretation about a particular observation open at any moment, even mutually exclusive ones, like your and your colleague's interpretation of the soft-spoken woman's difficulty getting heard in the conversation in the example above. Holding multiple interpretations in your head simultaneously is taxing, because our natural tendency is to always search for the one "right" answer. This mental balancing act requires the ability to view the same set of data from several different perspectives. An interpretation is only a guess, although the more you practice this activity, the better your guesses will be. Making your interpretation public is itself an intervention and often a provocative one. Making it tentatively, experimentally, and then watching (and then interpreting) the reaction can help you gauge how close to the mark you came.

If a leader has practiced the actions listed earlier as well as embrace the four dimensions of adaptive leadership, what kind of leadership traits can be expected of them? Adaptive leaders who have practiced their skill sets tend to have a fluency in connecting everyday work and initiatives with the core values and objectives of the overall organization. Other than just encouraging calculated risk-taking, adaptive leaders also have the emotional empathy to understand that change takes time, requires commitment, and is faced with occasional bumps and scrapes. That same emotional acuity allows an adaptive leader to embrace mistakes both made by themselves and by team members. And when dealing with macro level experiences, adaptive leaders understand that large-scale change is different from medium-scale change, which in turn is different from day-to-day change initiatives. But above all, adaptive leaders foster an environment where change is a part of daily activity (Corporate Finance Institute 2018).

Essential Traits of Effective Change Agents

There are many views on what is needed to effectively lead change. This section is our compilation of some of the key attributes based on the experiences of the leaders we interviewed and our research from our book *Leaderocity*[TM]: *Leading at the Speed of Now* (Dool 2021). It is not meant to be an exhaustive list but more of a set of foundational (core) attributes that each leader can leverage to enhance or extend their change agency competency.

There is a difference between "traditional leaders" and the "collaborative leaders" need in this era ("the speed of now"). The themes of teaming, communication, collaboration, and facilitation weave and intersect in the collaborate leadership style. We propose that this collaborative style is more effective for leaders to be effective change agents.

Team-B (2015) offered this comparison. Figure 6.1 highlights some of the differences between traditional leadership practices and the move towards a more collaborative approach.

Research and experience offer a set of personal traits that effective change leaders seem to embody. Table 6.2 highlights some essential personal leadership traits needed to be an effective change leader in this chaotic environment.

Sinek (2019) notes that if we approach change with a "infinite" mindset, in other words, as an event or program, it will lead to all kinds of potential dysfunctions including a decline in trust, collaboration, and innovation. He argues that in times of continuous change (the infinite game), leading with an infinite mindset will move the organization in a better direction. He makes the point that an infinite mindset will help a company thrive in good times and survive tougher times by infusing resilience into the organizational DNA. Leaders with an infinite mindset want to build an organization that embraces surprises and adapts with them.

Montague and Ryan from *co:collective* offer an approach to communicating change which they call "StoryDoing" (Kelley 2016).

They argue that having a clear and distinctive change story is critical in the dynamic environment facing leaders today. They make the point that is not enough to have the story and communicating it, leaders also have to live it.

They posit that "StoryDoing" is essential, placing the change story at the center of the organization and organizing around

Figure 6.1 Leadership evolving to a more collaborative style

it will make the difference between a good organization and a great one.

They offer these elements for "StoryDoing":

- Start with a Quest
  - A good quest defines the ambition for the organization, it captures the narrative and purpose of the organization. It is something everyone in the organization can rally around and adopt.

Table 6.2 Essential personal traits for effective change leaders

Essential Personal Traits	
Courageous	Change can be hard and leaders need to have courage of conviction to see it through. They need backbone and a willingness to go first and navigate the naysayers who inevitably surface. Embarking on change means choosing at times uncertainty and discomfort. As a change agent, you're also creating those conditions for others, which might not be popular. It takes courage to break out of the norm and to speak out to people who may not want to hear the truth.
Optimistic	Change creates stress and natural inertia will seek to fight it. Leaders need to be present change in a positive light, "we can do this" but also be grounded with doses of realism and pragmatism.
Patient	Change usually takes longer than expected and one of the main reasons for change "failures" is leadership impatience. Leaders need to be patient to see the change through and to fully embed it. They need to avoid the "serial change" syndrome by shifting too quickly.
Resilient	Virtually, no change initiative will go as planned; they is always some drift as conditions change or some highs and lows as the change is manifested. Leaders need to stay the course and not overreact to the inevitable highs and lows. Effective change agents don't take the lows or resistance personally. Instead, they bounce back and don't quit when they hear "no." Resilience enables the persistence required to drive change.
Deliberate	Change leaders need to be strategic, intentional, and deliberate. Change is a leader-led process. to influence change, you must deliberately choose the words and actions that break the patterns so change can happen. Change leaders need to take on a persona of being calm, confident, and in control.
Empathetic	Change agents must be able to put themselves in other people's shoes to understand their experience. You must predict how people will feel about change even if you don't feel that way. Empathy stops you from judging people for resisting change, so you can recognize that their response to change is normal and valid. Effective change agents help employees understand what's in it for them and use that to drive buy-in.
Grit	Angela Duckworth argues that an individual's grit is a better predictor of long-term success, more than talent or IQ. Grit is a combination of passion and perseverance for long-term goals. She notes, "I do mean hard work and not quitting things when they're hard, but I also mean passion." Change leaders need to have some grit to overcome the obstacles that likely will emerge. Dweck (2016) defined it as a growth mindset, the resilience that makes a leader determined to bounce back from failures and setbacks.
Flexible	We call this "focused flexibility," meaning that leaders need to stick to the change vision and plan, but also be flexible enough to adapt as conditions warrant. They have to be committed to their change vision but too much in love with it. They have to actively monitor the change initiative and be willing shift when it warrants—shifting both too early or too late can have unintended consequences.

- Starts with the CEO
  - Employees will not fully commit to a quest unless they sense the full commitment of the leadership team. The senior leaders must champion and live the quest consistently. Gary Hamel noted: "Today, no leader can afford to be indifferent to the challenge of engaging employees in the work of creating the future. Engagement may have been optional in the past, but it is the whole game today" (Kelley 2016).
- Organizations build their story into their culture
  - StoryDoing organizations don't tell their story as much as live it. They express it through every action they take.
- Organizations are organized by shared purpose
  - They build their story into everything they do. They imagine their future based on their quest and this becomes the blueprint for organizing.

Adaptive Leadership Teams

While an adaptive leader embodying all the characteristics and traits that we described previously are critically important, in today's modern corporate structure, leadership teams and team dynamics have an influence on corporate culture as well. Penetration of leadership attitudes through an entire organization is extremely critical to creating an adaptable organization. The best ways to communicate adaptable behavior is by modeling that behavior with the leadership team at large. While team dynamics can take a variety of forms, reviewed in the frame of adaptability, there are some clear team characteristics that engender an overall adaptive mindset. Some characteristics come about by the agenda set by the leader, namely, encouraging distributed leadership, picking the right members of the team and providing a clear direction to the team members on what needs to be achieved. On the other hand, something as elemental as trust needs to be built within the team and while it can be set in motion by the leader, it needs to be developed within the team itself (Torres and Rimmer 2011).

Torres and Rimmer (2011) continue their work to identify the five traits of the leadership team that are critical in maintaining an adaptable atmosphere. Specifically, they list the ability for teams to work with one voice, the ability to use multiple options to identify solutions to a problem, the ability to synthesize a considerable amount of data, a commitment to working within agreed-upon boundaries, and the ability to work between silos verticals and horizontals. Some of these traits overlap with those expected of the leader themselves. Conversely, is important to note that there are some of these traits that need to be developed over time and in group, thus reasserting the fact that a leader's work is equal parts individual and group related. It is natural to conclude that in some ways, the traits of a leader and the traits of a leadership team overlap based on the characteristics mentioned in this and previous chapters. When leadership teams are in sync with the leader, the team itself can start to reflect a combined effort, focus, and voice that will reflect well across an organization. Leaders that have been able to bring their leadership teams along to this unified status are more likely to succeed with their agenda, direction, and overall cultural course setting for the company at large.

Challenges of Adaptive Leadership

While adaptable leadership is indeed a sought after and critical part of today's business, there are some shortcomings, both in the ability to attain adaptability and issues with being adaptable in and of itself. Some of the root challenges for an adaptive leader can be found in the chapter in this book on organizational adaptability, namely, if a leader is adaptable but the organization is not in lockstep with that attitude, problems are likely to ensue. Consequently, adaptability leads to rapid change and if the organization at large is unable to acknowledge the need for these changes while also respecting the work that was done before, it is likely a leader will have a subset of employees that are unhappy with the change to status quo. Finally, as previously discussed, while distributed leadership sounds like a great idea, in practice, many organizations are not ready to make that leap. Organizational, cultural, individual, and social norms might contribute to an expectation that the leadership make all the decisions. Changing a culture to one that celebrates distributed decision making is a process best done with care and over time (Indeed 2021). All of this feeds into the overall theme that change is a heavily human and management reality, so for an adaptive leader to be effect, they must prioritize their employees and middle management. By bringing the people within an organization on board with the overall vision, allowing them say and participation in developing that vision, and then having the trust to distribute responsibility for change to others all are likely to be success factors in countering the challenges to adaptive leadership.

CHAPTER 7

The Adaptive Organization

Brower (2020) frames the need to lead change effectively and to embed adaptability into the organization's DNA:

> Given that today's business context is in constant flux, the ability of an organization to change and adapt is an ongoing effort. Rather than a static process companies can get through and then move away from, it must be continuous and intentional. People who are flexible contribute to an organizational culture of adaptability, and this ability to shift and adjust must be developed for all employees and for teams—ultimately contributing to organizational capability.

The adaptive enterprise is defined as one that constantly senses changes in the environment and quickly adapts its strategies, processes, and operational tactics accordingly (Capgemini 2003). In this environment, firms must react to changes in the marketplace in real or near real time. The threats in the business environment have reached unprecedented proportions, particularly given the speed of consumer behavioral change and preferences in the 21st century. As observed by Patel (2015), one of the biggest reasons that 90 percent of startups fail is because of their inability to adapt to changes in the market, speed of growth, and the inability to pivot and recover from market force disruptions. One of the most evident cases of such inability to adapt is captured in the fall of Blockbuster, the video rental chain. A company that at its height had over 9,000 storefronts, most prefer to blame its demise on Netflix and the elimination of late fees. Yet the biggest driver of its failings was its inability to adapt and embrace new technologies, an almost dogmatic reliance on their core product (DVDs) and expansion of its footprint beyond profitability (Murphy 2019). These positions taken by Blockbuster are emblematic of a company that shunned change in favor of the status quo, or rather, their standing business model. Created from the need of the times and demands of customers, what it failed to do is to adapt to customer changes and preferences.

A key to becoming an adaptive enterprise is to reframe the notion of change. Instead of treating change as an unusual organizational response, change is reframed as a natural part of the organization's fabric. Change is repositioned as an organizational asset, allowing the organization to seamlessly adapt to changing conditions.

Sikora, Beaty, and Forward (2004) argue that change should be repositioned as an active verb instead of a noun. Reeves and Deimler (2011) posit that companies with managers that embed the idea of change in their employees' minds as natural and commonplace tend to foster rapid adaptation. Rapid experimentation, keeping a hawkish eye on weaknesses of competitors with an eye toward adapting at the slightest missteps have positioned several companies for success in this century. It is important to note that being adaptable flies in the face of how we commonly regard an established business—one that is stable and can churn out profit at a regular, predictable clip. There is a fine line here to consider—stability in internal politics, management, and incremental growth is distinctively different from a company that is adapting to external pressures and factors. A company can be simultaneously profit stable and environmentally adaptable. As Pulakos and Kaiser (2020) noted:

> Companies that are best able to bounce back from jolts and adjust have a stable foundation. It provides the confidence, security, and optimism people need to keep calm, act rationally, and swiftly adapt to disruptive change. There are seven evidence-based practices that leaders can use to build a stable organizational foundation on which employees and teams can find firm footing: sharpen your focus, break down barriers, optimize failure, build optimism, reassure people, harmonize resources, and preplan for recovery.

If an organization is to look at change as a verb and not as a noun, then paying attention to moments of change and embracing it is as important as the change itself. During the 2020 pandemic, companies that focused on the change at hand and chose not to press forward with preexisting plans tended to be the ones that survived the economic stall, no better evidenced by the pivoting of Zoom versus its competitors (Nivel 2020). As the likes of Skype for Business and Webex waited for customers to come to them, Zoom adapted in the moment of economic change, providing new developments, upgrades, and situation-based features that embraced the year's instability. In less than six months, Zoom increased it subscription base from 10 million to 300 million users. Lesser noticed but equally as adaptive was the pivoting displayed by Home Depot. Sensing an increase in home-related repairs and upgrades amid the pandemic lockdown, the home improvement giant embraced technology, secured supply changes, and pushed to become an essential service to keep its doors open (Loten 2020).

Of course, the adaptive enterprise is not immune from a macro-change event (e.g., merger or economic shock). These would have to be addressed directly. The adaptive organization's frame of reference is geared toward ecosystem integration and its execution focus moves past reacting to change or managing change to seamlessly adapting to change (see Figure 2 from Dool 2006). Figure 7.1 from Cap Gemini/Ernst & Young offers a path for an organization to adopt a more adaptive organizational approach.

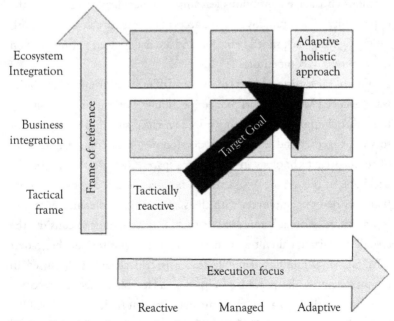

Figure 7.1 Adaptive organization frame of reference
Source: Adapted from Cap Gemini/Ernst & Young 2005

The adaptive enterprise would be better suited to reduce the negative impact of the frequent daily stressors, which seem to be a bigger source of employee stress. The point of the reframing of change is to create an environment where change becomes continuous and often takes place unintentionally as employees go about doing their jobs.

The Key to Adaptability: People and Mindset

The human element of a business is most frequently the area that is all at once the most and least capable of adapting. As observed by Uhl-Bien and Arena (2018): Leadership for organizational adaptability addresses how leaders can position organizations and its people within them to be adaptive in the face of complex challenges.

Taken to its core, companies that have flexible viewpoints on human resources give rise to an adaptable culture and environment (Do, Yeh, and Madsen 2016, 663). In fact, it is quite appropriate to identify adaptability as an overall competitive advantage, enabling an entire organization to not just be good at one thing, but rather to be able to pivot and learn how to do a multitude of things (Reeves and Deimler 2011). Such organizations encourage continuous learning, calculated risk taking, and the opportunity to fail. Employees have access to resources across the organization, fighting back siloed behavior, and are encouraged to capitalize on the weakness of competitors.

One of the earliest adopters of this kind of innovation and adaptability was Lockheed Martin and its pioneering Skunk Works team. Responding to market competition, the company encouraged small teams of scientist to work together and take on the development and commercialization of competitive technology in the aircraft space (Gwynne 1997, 19). The backbone of the Skunk Works teams, however, was a corporate culture that provided the employees with the space and risk tolerance necessary to unlock the adaptable mindset. As such, it is important to consider the overall organizational culture and not just the disposition of the leader/ CEO alone. While an adaptable leader is critical and is discussed in another chapter, the pervasive culture of adaptable *leadership* needs to make its way through as much of the management ranks as possible. One leader alone cannot create a Skunk Works atmosphere; several leaders and managers need to identify the team, release the potential, and provide continuous encouragement to attain an adaptability mindset.

Creating an Adaptable Organization

The literature tends to vary about the best ways to create an organizational culture that demonstrates an ability and readiness to be adaptable to external and internal changes. The recommendations change depending on size of organization, cultural and societal working norms, and the point in time when the research was conducted. However, almost all recommendations seem to be universal on the investment, development, and mindset shift needed of the employees, leadership, and mid-level managers. Drawing a line across the most common recommendations for workers to become adaptable, we are able to come up with some common themes.

Leadership Encourages Experimentation, Innovation, and Cross-Vertical Communication

Static organizations with silos are already well-known characteristics of challenging workplace cultures. One of the few research studies available using a historical measure to identify characteristics of long-term adaptable organizations was conducted by Costanza, Blacksmith, Coats, Severt, and DeCostanza (2016). Using a regression analysis, their analysis of 95 highly successful organizations all pointed toward the conclusion that companies that embrace change internally and respond to change externally are most likely to survive the test of time. A central guiding force for internal change readiness is the existing of a culture of experimentation and innovation. As observed by Heifetz, Linsky, and Grashow (2009),

> People who make mistakes or experiment with new ways of doing things are not marginalized. Instead, they are treated as founts of wisdom because they have had experiences that the organization needs to capture. For example, at one global bank, the CEO regularly identifies those responsible for big mistakes, helps them tease out what they have learned, and then sends them around the world sharing their new knowledge with colleagues.

To some degree, this can be regarded as the different between a carrot or stick approach to failure and learning. Inflexible organizations tend to punish mistakes and make examples of individuals as cautionary tales. The adaptive organization knows when to identify the difference between a mistake made by innovative effort versus a mistake made from negligence. The latter can cause cultural issues if fostered and supported while the former will help build an environment where innovation receives encouragement regardless to success or failure.

Innovation is also fostered when leadership encourages an environment with limited restrictions and rule setting. Stalwart dedication to process and organizational rules are as limiting as setting structure to the work of painters and sculptures—if a blank slate is not available to creators, then the outcomes to a degree are predefined. As observed by the American Management Association (2019),

> The foundation of any bottom-up transformation starts with the empowerment of self-motivated, self-directed teams. An abundance of structure and rule-setting tends to inhibit creativity and adaptiveness, particularly when the structure is hierarchical, the default organizational form for many prior to today's knowledge era. In the experience of many of the participants, the most effective collaboration is voluntary, informal, self-supervised. Good personal relationships lead to successful collaboration as it's hard to collaborate with people with whom you are "commanded" to work. "By mandate" teams have a hard time looking at their environment with an open mind—familiar assumptions and conventional approaches come to the fore. Smaller, self-generating groups are freer to challenge the dominant paradigms and arrive at new ways of adapting to emerging challenges and opportunities.

The association goes on to identify the importance of intellectual safe harbor spaces, where new methods of creation and thinking are welcome and allowed to flourish (2019). Critical to the success of such groups is leadership's willingness to review and hear of the outcomes of such teams. The absence of leadership in seeing the outputs of these teams displays only a perfunctory interest in the environment that has been created—lip service to the process but no interest in the outcomes. Leadership involvement should ideally be in place from the beginning— creating the space, picking the team, communicating expectations, continuous encouragement, and a willingness to review outcomes and encourage further experimentation.

Another important facet of adaptive teams is their ability to share information across business areas, thus breaking down silo-based think-ing and behaviors. Adaptive teams are able to move seamlessly "both horizontally across roles and vertically to connect with the next level of leadership down from them" (Torres and Rimmer 2011). Bucking tra-ditional business models, this allows teams to go to where the need is most. For example, IT teams are able to work seamlessly with HR teams depending on the project. Typical sentiments of "this is my area, do not touch" are no longer part of the dialogue, but rather taken as opportu-nities to learn from each other. As observed by Hope, Bunce, and Röösli (2011), one of the best ways to achieve this level of communication and transparency is to ensure that all teams keep the end customer in focus throughout the innovation process. With one unified driving force, tra-ditional notions of territorialism around one's work area will begin to dissipate. These kinds of "…innovative management models represent the only remaining source of sustainable competitive advantage" (Hope, Bunce, and Röösli 2011).

Flexibility in Decision Making

One of the most commonly cited traits of flexible organizations is the idea of distributed leadership and governance. The origins of distributed lead-ership date back to the early 1950s but did not come into wider adoption until three decades later (Gronn 2002). As observed by Spillane (2012), distributed leadership is both the act of leadership decisions being shared among leaders as well as the continuous act of communicating between leaders on a regular basis. Applied to an adaptive organization, leaders communicate the clear direction of the organization while yielding day-to-day and project-based details to team leaders across the enterprise. Viewed from the opposite angle, rigid organizations tend to be strongly focused on the "heroics" of the leader rather than collective innovation and thinking (Spillane 2012). In his book on the topic, Schneeweiss (2012) used a plethora of examples to show that all types of decisions—marketing, supply chain, quantitative—can be benefited from allowing decision makers to work together both vertically and horizontally based on their project needs and objectives. Such companies tend to "…believe frontline employees have the best understanding of customers, suppliers and production machines. Therefore, frontline employees should make most of the decisions" (Minaar 2020). Mallon (2020) shared the following real-life example of adaptation to distributed decision making:

> As an example, at one global pharmaceutical company, decisions about resources and project prioritization had historically been made piecemeal, with the leaders of the R&D, marketing, legal, and compliance functions signing off on their "piece" of the decision, followed by the CEO reviewing and approving the decision—in this case, to move on to the next step in the drug development process—as a whole. This practice of pooling individual decisions for the CEO's ultimate signoff was not only slow—many decisions were delayed as their individual components made their way up the chain of command—but also did not allow the functional leaders to take each other's perspectives into account. To speed the decision-making process, the organization identified what decisions had to be made, determined which ones were most critical to the outcomes they cared about, and analyzed how these decisions were currently being made. They then assigned decision-making accountability to specific people or cross-functional groups, highlighting decisions for which they deemed it essential to bring cognitive diversity—diversity of thought—to foster innovation and get drugs to market more quickly.

Mallon goes on to observe that one of the biggest barriers to organizations of embracing this management philosophy is the desire of C-suite leaders to retain control. Since these leaders were entrusted with the future of the organization, it is somewhat natural for them to be reticent to distributed decision making. But as we shall see in the next section, the happy middle ground that embraces adaptability is attain by relying on C-suite leadership on setting the overall goals, objectives, and guiding principles while allowing frontline works to innovate, decide, and embrace flexible. In the previous example, we see this mutually beneficial environment playing out—setting out clear parameters or limits while allowing for significant autonomy within those barriers.

Organizational Common Goals

The value of setting a common shared goal across an organization or across parts of an organization have been widely studied with a variety of benefits and techniques. The importance of common goals within the context of an adaptive organization is critical to maintain a united focus amid distributed leadership, innovation, and flexibility. The need for common goals have become even more important in a pandemic world where workforces for many companies are now physically separated. As observed by Torres and Rimmer (2011), leadership teams with exercise the use of defined goals and the use of metrics to maintain accountability of actions, all predicated on mutual trust. They go on to share:

> Adaptive teams take the time to get completely aligned about the organization's vision, values, and vital priorities, while respecting individual differences of opinion and experience. Once a diverse team has reached agreement, members have the same "true north" guiding their strategic moves, and they display an absolute consistency in articulating that direction. Rather than demanding that employees follow a rules-based script that quickly grows out of date, leaders focus on transmitting the expected outcomes that can help steer the organization through any eventuality and allow experimentation to occur (Torres and Rimmer 2011).

Common goals centered around mutual success also allows for a commonly shared means of measuring success. Companies that measure results from sales, buyer satisfaction, and outcomes will have the data needed to keep the teams within the organizational adaptable by using real data (Holland 2016). For example, adaptable teams as narrated above will be constantly changing to environmental inputs and competition activity.

This kind of adaptability should certainly be encouraged, however, being flexible for the sake of flexibility alone without examining results will quickly result in creating an organization that develops thoughtful products or services that no buyer is interested in.

A recent example of a product with great innovative origins in a distributed organization with common goals is the story of Google Glasses. The product had all the facets of a Google product—smart, innovative, sleek with all the bells and whistles typically associated with a high-tech device. Yet one of the biggest postmortem consensuses on why the product failed is that it was a child of smart developers who did not think through to what the actual use of the product would be, or namely, a failure to take into account that there was limited interest in the marketplace for a such a device (Yoon 2018). Yoon goes on to identify that there was a lack of common understanding by the developers at Google as to how to best use the device. Without this common goal, they proceeded with the assumption that the innovative level of the product alone would help it sell. They also lacked a consensus on what added value it gave to customers. In the absence of measurable expectations of innovative development, products like the Google Glasses have come through the innovation lab but landed flat on the innovation floor. In fact, having a clear definition of what can be judged as innovative needs to be made clear to all development teams within a company. Whirlpool, for example, states that "… for a product or service to be counted as innovative…it must be unique and compelling to the consumer, create a competitive advantage, sit on a migration path that can yield further innovations, and provide consumers with more value than anything else in the market" (Hamel and Tennant 2015).

Equal to definitions and common goals is the need to also measure outcomes from these common goals. Establishing regular known performance indicators (KPIs), regular metrics, and productivity check-ins and measuring outputs and results may sound like a laborious set of expectations reminiscent of strict management principles. However, the importance of such measures is to ensure that everyone stays on the path of their articulated common goals, measures to productivity of innovation, and in the event that such efforts are not productive, be ready to innovate the *way* you innovate. Hamel and Tennant (2015) provide a useful set of innovation measures that are applicable to many teams:

- Inputs: the investment dollars and employee time devoted to innovation, along with the number of ideas that are generated internally each month or sourced from customers, suppliers, and other outsiders.
- Throughputs: the number and quality of ideas that enter the pipeline after initial screening, the time it takes for those ideas to move from concept to prototype to reality, and the notional value of the innovation pipeline.
- Outputs: the number of innovations that reach the market in a given period, the percentage of revenue derived from new products and services, and the margin gains that are attributable to innovation.
- Leadership: the percentage of executive time that gets devoted to mentoring innovation projects, and 360-degree survey results that reveal the extent to which executives are exhibiting pro-innovation behaviors.
- Competence: the percentage of employees who have been trained as business innovators, the percentage of employees who have qualified as innovation "black belts," and changes in the quality of ideas that are being generated across the firm.
- Climate: the extent to which the firm's management processes facilitate or frustrate innovation, and the progress that is being made in removing innovation blockages.
- Efficiency: changes over time in the ratio of innovation outputs to inputs.
- Balance: the mix of different types of innovation (product, service, pricing, distribution, operations, etc.); different risk categories (incremental improvements versus speculative ventures); and different time horizons.

Efforts such as these help establish a baseline for innovative excellence. With some or all of these guidelines in place, an organization will truly be able to embrace systemic and systematic change without wasting effort on innovative for the same innovation.

Agile, innovative, responsive, nimble, creative, flexible—this is how organizations are described will succeed in the "speed of now" (Kelley 2016). This is the essence of embedding adaptability.

> Organizations that successfully embed change capability into the fabric of the organization will develop a competitive advantage. An agile organization has more strategic insight into human capital strategy and the workforce capabilities needed to execute strategy rapidly and effectively.

> *Responsiveness to change = competitive advantage*

Kelley (2016) offers six ways to embed adaptability into the fabric of the organization:

1. Equip leaders and staff with solid change skills and embed them in competency training.
2. Infuse change principles into job descriptions and hiring guidelines to ensure change-capable staff are hired and trained.
3. Ensure change language is embedded in value statements to clearly communicate the importance of adaptability.
4. Ensure change principles are built into goal setting and recognition programs.
5. Train staff to ensure they can recognize change resistance and can self-correct.
6. Communicate clearly and consistently how employees can contribute to the purpose of the organization. Connecting "why" with adaptability to ensure employees can see how they can directly contribute while also being agile.

Sibbet and Wendling (2018) offered seven challenges of change that also support the notion of embedding adaptability into the organizational culture. They also serve to frame our suggested new Change Leadership Framework (C^6) that follows.

Challenge One: Activating Awareness
Challenge Two: Engaging Change Leaders
Challenge Three: Creating and Sharing Possibilities
Challenge Four: Stepping into a New, Shared Vision
Challenge Five: Empowering Visible Actions
Challenge Six: Integrating Systemic Change
Challenge Seven: Sustaining Long Term

O'Reilly (Sibbet and Wendling 2018) argues that leaders and organizations need to be "ambidextrous." Leaders need to have the breadth of insight and flexibility to be effective in the current environment. They become the fuel that drives adaptability.

CHAPTER 8

The Change Mindset

Embedding adaptability into the natural processes of the organization will be largely dependent on also embedding a change mindset into the organization's core values and DNA. In this section, we further explore the change mindset through the elements of systems thinking, resilience, grit as well as a revisit of change resistance.

McKinsey & Company (Keller and Schaninger) (2019) made the point that "the need to shift mind-sets is the biggest block to successful transformations. The key lies in making the shift both individual and institutional—at the same time."

> In human systems, they help to achieve the same effect as the transformation of a caterpillar into a butterfly or a tadpole into a frog: when employees become open to new ways of looking at what's possible for them and their organization, they can never return to a state of not having that broader perspective, just as butterflies and frogs can't revert to their previous physical forms. To achieve such a metamorphosis, leaders must first identify the limiting mind-sets, then reframe them appropriately, and finally make sure that employees don't revert to earlier forms of behavior.
>
> Hamel and Prahalad also noted a wider truth about organizational life—namely, that mind-sets ingrained by past management practices remain ingrained far beyond the existence of the practices that formed them, even when new management practices have been put in place.
>
> These often lead to "root-cause" mindsets. The key is to reframe these beliefs and expand the range of reasonable behavioral choices employees can make, day in and day out.

There is also the need to reshape the work environment (Keller and Schaninger 2019):

> Victor Frankl summed up, in a compelling way, the full picture of what it takes to achieve caterpillar-to-butterfly-like personal change when he wrote: "Between stimulus and response there is a space. In that space is our power to choose our response." We find it helpful to use a shorthand version of Frankl's idea: S (stimulus) + T (how you choose to think about the stimulus) = R (response).
>
> The S in this equation is vital for the aforementioned work on the T to fully take hold: the work environment is a particularly powerful shaper of employee mind-sets and behavior, albeit a relatively slow-acting one.
>
> When it comes to changing the stimulus (the S)—the work environment—employees are exposed to, we find that the four levers in McKinsey's "influence model" offer the most practical and proven guide (below). Research and experience demonstrate that changes in thinking and behaving will be significant and sustained if leaders and employees see clear communications and rituals (the *understanding and conviction* lever); if supporting incentives, structures, processes, and systems are in place (the *formal-mechanisms* lever); if training and development opportunities are combined with sound talent decisions (the *confidence and skills* lever); and if senior leaders and influence leaders allow others to take their cues from the leaders' own behavior (the *role-modeling* lever).

These elements will help embed the change mindset within teams and organizations. It is important to remember that the change mindset needs to be embodied throughout the organization. A strategy for an organizational leader can be to begin the socialization and adoption of a change mindset first with middle management at large. Suffice it to say, if middle management adopts the levers mentioned above, then the role-modeling behavior will have a multiplier effect throughout the organization, thereby reducing time between the stimulus added and the response expected. For example, if considerable time and attention is given by a CEO in sharing, transferring, and encouraging a change mindset among the senior team, then the senior team is more likely to adopt the change mindset and pass it on throughout the organization. A leader who edicts change without bringing managers "on board" with the change is likely to be limitedly successful in encouraging a mindset shift. As previously discussed, transparency and continuous reminders of the reason and method of change (the formal-mechanisms lever) will give the organization the greatest chance of long-term change that "sticks."

The "influence model" is a practical and proven guide for changing the mind-sets and behavior of employees.

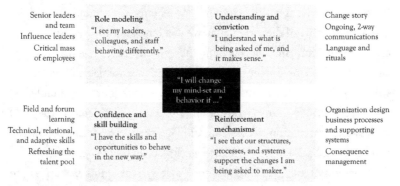

Source: McKinsey & Company (2019)

Westover (2020) noted that in essence, good organizational change and development require a systems-thinking mindset and an interdisciplinary, holistic approach to tackling complex organizational challenges.

Six Themes of Systems Thinking

Although systems thinking may be considered a talent, there is a lot of supportive theory and a stack of tools to use when applying it. Leyla Acaroglu, a systems-thinking educator, points out six key elements to creating a systems thinking mindset: (1) interconnectedness, (2) synthesis, (3) emergence, (4) feedback loops, (5) causality, and (6) systems mapping.

Interconnectedness and synthesis relate to the dynamic relationships between various parts of a whole, the process of obtaining expected synergies between parts of the company. This includes the idea of circularity, which stresses the requirement of a mindset shift from linear to circular. Similarly, the concept of emergence relates to the outcomes of synergies that can come about as the elements of a system interact with each other in nonlinear ways. In the workplace, this often takes the form of the push and pull that happens due to organizational politics and competing priorities. Organizational leaders with a systems-thinking mindset will see this as an opportunity for enhanced collaborations and innovation.

Balancing and reinforcing feedback loops within an organization serve as guidance for making adjustments as we learn more about the interconnectedness of the elements of the system and their outcomes. Additionally, causality refers to the flows of influence between the many interconnected parts within a system. As we better understand the casualty and directionality of these elements, we will have an improved perspective on the many fundamental parts of the system, including relationships and feedback loops. In the workplace, a skilled systems-thinking leader will ensure that mechanisms for multiple feedback loops are established and effectively communicated to their employees. Furthermore, they will understand correlation versus causation as they use the data gathered from the feedback loops to enhance workplace practices.

Finally, systems mapping is a tool that systems thinkers can use to identify and visually map out the many interrelated elements of a complex system, which will help them "develop interventions, shifts, or policy decisions that will dramatically change the system in the most effective way," as Acaroglu explains it. By visually laying out the key inputs and outputs, all of the stakeholders and the directions of the flows of information and influence, you can visually start to see and more deeply understand the nonlinear complexity of the given system, which can help you make appropriate adjustments to workplace policy, practice, and associated systems in your organization.

Contemporary businesses operate in ecosystems full of interconnectedness and constant feedback loops. Mapping such complex systems helps organizational leaders navigate into adaptive strategies. The ultimate gain is the ability of organizations to be responsive to the changes in ecosystems and to be prepared to fine-tune and adapt parts of their organization on the fly. With this understanding, systems thinking provides clear benefits to organizations. It helps in framing complex problems, which are often being misdiagnosed when using linear thinking. It shows alternative directions for improvement with respect to the company's inner and outer connections. It gives a significant advantage in increasing the organization's capacity for change and, as a consequence, to fulfill the vision of business sustainability. Although it requires some talent and a deeper understanding of complexity and ambiguity, systems thinking can be successfully introduced and utilized to strengthen organizations.

Resilience

Resilience is the ability to bounce back from a difficult challenge or from a less than positive experience. Resilience allows employees and the organization to face a problem or challenge, overcome it, become more confident, adaptable, and wiser from the associated learnings. Because change is so engrained in this "speed of now" environment, leaders need to find ways to embed resilience in the organization.

This starts with awareness. Leaders need to be aware of how the organization and staff typically respond to change. Insights (n.d.) notes that most staff handle many relatively small changes on a daily basis and manage to keep making it through their days relatively unscathed; but if leaders stop to pay attention, they will notice that all these changes have an impact on staff. We may also notice that change impacts staff members differently.

For some people change is an energizer, a motivator; in fact, these people may seek out change and appear to thrive on change. For other people, it is just the opposite, and change is experienced as exhausting and demotivating, something to put up with and be endured.

Knowing how change affects the organization and staff can help determine the change strategies that will allow the organization to be resilient in the face of the often constant changes we face.

Proctor (2020) notes:

> The real value of resilience for organizations lies in the ability to successfully implement business imperatives. Most change projects fail because the people involved are just not resilient enough to deal with the perpetual change loading—where change projects

continue to be undertaken without any assessment of whether the change capacity exists to deliver them successfully in the organization. And our research continues to tell us that people are feeling overwhelmed by change—in fact, even before recent levels of disruption 48% of people felt their own organization was facing too much change.

Proctor (2020) offers seven key characteristics of resilient people (see the figure below):

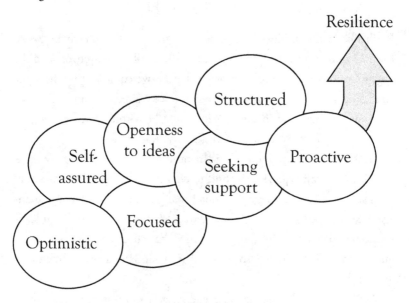

1. Optimistic: Resilient people believe that change will have a positive outlook. They are able to analyze even an apparently dire situation in a way that gives them hope for the future.
2. Self-assured: Resilient people have a strong but realistic belief in their own capabilities. As a result, they tend to control change, rather than the change controlling them.
3. Focused: Resilient people have the focus needed to be able to prioritize activities effectively. They can pursue goals successfully, even in the face of adversity.
4. Open to ideas: Resilient people have an open mind to different tactics and strategies. They tend to be good at generating alternative approaches and solutions to match the changing situation.

5. Seek support: Resilient people actively seek the support of others during times of change. They look for opportunities to involve the skills and experience of other people as well as their own.

6. Structured: Resilient people are able to analyze the situation and create an effective plan to implement change, with enough flexibility built in to cope with the shifting situation.

7. Proactive: Resilient people are prepared to step out into the "unknown" and take the action necessary to make change.

Akins (2020) notes: "Resilience is the ability to adapt well in the face of threat, adversity or significant stress. A critical survival element to assimilate to ongoing change, resilience allows oneself to bounce back after hardship."

In the face of fluctuating regulations, disruptive competitors, and emergent client requirements, learning professionals and people leaders can employ five strategies to build resilience:

1. **Steward your mind and emotions**

   Change is a journey to a place you and your peers have never been before. This is risky business. Rather than moving straight from current state to goal state, the path of change curves with emotional dips, including fear and anger, as employees leave the status quo behind for the great unknown. People often take change personally. Fueling this emotional dip, per the NeuroLeadership Institute, is a sense of social threat—fear of how the change will impact oneself and their interactions with others. In today's age of blurred lines between life and work, employees take into further consideration how professional changes will affect their personal life and choices, thereby increasing the feeling of threat to the status quo on both planes. Without a growth mindset, new and uncharted paths increase that sense of threat.

   Take for example the omnipresent dialogue in most workplaces in 2021—to telecommute or to return to the traditional office, in part or in whole. This discussion has hit a crescendo like never before and, given its change implications, has caused due and undue stress to employees who feel this is as much an infringement of personal choices as it is of the workplace. As previously discussed, our world has blurred the lines between the personal and the professional. The flexibility that comes from "working from home"—be it perceived or real—speaks to the core of why change going forward is likely to almost always strike to a personal emotional point for employees and leaders alike.

The growth mindset, characterized by Dr. Carol Dweck as a bent toward true learning, includes a willingness to embrace challenge and persist through adversity—qualities essential for successfully navigating change. As you travel through the change curve, allow for progress rather than perfection. Individuals with growth mindsets stretch themselves, accept feedback, and take the long view. An openness to hard work, risk, and even the prospect of failure provide foundational aspects for cultivating change resilience. Developing these traits take time within a team and organization at large. For example, an organization with a previous leader who was not open to failure and learning will struggle with a new leader eager to take the fail and learn approach to growth. Even when expressly stated by leadership as a preferred new way to work, most employees will take time to trust that failure will be embraced as a means of constant improvement. Endemic to this, once again, is the reality today that work and life are deeply intertwined. What was previously only a risk on the professional front is not a risk to both profession and personal life.

To develop a growth mindset, become aware of the personal narrative in your head. If you notice that you quickly approach problems with fixed answers or solutions, open yourself up to alternatives. During times of challenge, speak statements that make room for growth. For example, if a new opportunity is bungled, rather than remarking, "Wow, that was really bad," try saying, "Guess I am not there quite yet. I need more practice." Allowing for growth relieves pressure and enables you to set appropriate expectations. Repetition and constant reinforcement of this new mindset is key as employees might see this as only incidental or part of the beginning of change, reverting to their old behaviors. While at times it may seem to a leader as overkill, providing constant, predictable, and continuous reinforcement of the new mindset will provide a sense of stability amid a lot of change.

Through their words and actions, leaders either communicate a sense of hope for the future or foster stress and fear. The most effective leaders of change develop their emotional intelligence in order to leverage the power of positivity as they move their people through change. Emotions are contagious, so be careful what you spread. Similarly, consider multiple vehicles of communication. In a hybrid work environment, relying solely on communicating in-person might at first seem more personal and emotionally open, but it does not take account of modern methods of communication. The modern leader will communicate with employees and middle management by embracing in-person, e-mail, social, and corporate online networks as a multiprong means of communicating while also adding personal opportunities for connection outside of work. While this may seem all encompassing and at times overwhelming to leadership, it is quickly becoming a staple of leadership in C-suite board rooms.

2. **Exert agency by taking action**

Agency, as defined by the social sciences, is the capacity of individuals to act independently and make their own choices. Taking self-directed action, or exerting agency, can lower one's threat meter.

When experiencing change, start by asking yourself what you can control in the present situation. For example, in the case of a reorganization, you might familiarize yourself with new org charts, meet your new boss, and discover their vision, recall how your personal strengths have served you through past changes and tailor your experience to align with the new environment.

Even in situations where you have little or no control, you can find actions that move you toward small wins. At the very least, determine to control your response to change by beginning with your attitude. Do you need to come to terms with the change by practicing acceptance? Aim to get comfortable being uncomfortable. Comfortable is nice, but it's not a necessity.

As a learning leader, help employees exert their agency by giving them opportunities to weigh in on strategies for managing the change at hand. Give team members options when possible and invite them to think creatively and take ownership of the change journey. Once again, repetition and modeled behavior is the key here. One of declarations or invitations for input followed by little to no additional invitations will open a leader up to questions of resolve and throughput. By taking action on a continuous basis, you are able to reinforce the change as the newly adapted normal.

3. **Clarify the why and create a way**

   Understanding the why behind a change helps secure a sense of purpose and set a shared strategy. It is important to know the organizational rationale for change and be able to share it with your team. On a personal level, discover how the organizational "why" aligns with your personal why—your vision, values, and purpose. This enables you to honor yourself and your principles in a world of change. In this speed of now world, employees not only consume information around the "why" at a rapid pace, they are also able to compare and contrast change initiatives with their personal and professional networks outside your organization. As such, a competitive advantage to have is to be able to gain the confidence of your employees by being transparent about the "why." At the same time, a distinction should be made in your mind about how you explain the "why"; this does not need to be a justification of your decision process. Rather, it is meant to be a rationale for how the changes will benefit the business, and thus "why" the changes are taking place.

   Beyond why, you need a way. The way is not a detailed how-to but a broad overview of where you are heading and how you plan to get there. The Heath brothers call this a "destination postcard." You don't need to know all the turns, but you do need to know you are going to California—not New York or Chicago. As a learning leader, this means identifying the most important actions while leaving room to work through the details later. Having a sense of where you are going and why you are moving in that direction combats concerns that escalate change fatigue. In the absence of explaining the way in which you are achieving this and the why, employees and middle management will be left to fill in the blanks of rationale on their own. This is likely to contribute to erroneous and at worst, false narratives for your presumptively well thought out direction.

By way of illustration, as part of a global training project sponsored by the Department of State, a group of international government and nongovernmental organization (NGO) leaders from a developing country worked together with experts in the United States to expand their understanding of governance, transparency, and citizen participation. The intent was that, upon their return home, these leaders would further develop these capacities in their country. Trust between government and the new NGO entity was fledgling, so they began to identify the rationale for working together that made sense to both groups, illustrating the value of NGO work and the benefit of government partnership. The U.S. team provided guiding principles like collaboration, minimal force, and checks and balances. Then they identified some critical actions to get them on their way. With access to local programs, the global leaders saw firsthand how police, the legal system, and nonprofits collaborate to address issues such as domestic violence.

A year after the project, the team learned that a training program for an entire division of their federal police force was rewritten to implement these principles in the participants' home country. This solution could not have been prescribed initially. By clarifying the why and creating a way that provided a general direction and identified critical moves, the international leaders could do the rest.

4. **Coach by leaning in**

Reframe resistance. Resistance—the refusal to accept or comply with someone or something—is normal, and it is not necessarily negative. It indicates that people need more time, information, or support to process the change. That is where your role as coach comes in. Rather than trying to avoid or squelch resistance, leaders who foster change resilience lean in and investigate the reasons for resistance. The primary mode for investigating the source and reasoning for the resistance should be to listen and complete a thorough intake. Presumptions in resistance situations create more issues and make it difficult to bring everyone "onboard" with change.

Consider your reaction when a team member expresses uncertainty or a lack of support to change. Are you quick to defend, or do you explore their reluctance? Often, what looks like resistance is an expression of concern rising from their commitment. In order to coach your team through the change, you must first understand where they are coming from.

Ask more questions and make fewer statements. Have transparent, one-on-one conversations. Be curious and adopt an attitude of openness—contributing to a sense of equity. As The Change Lab recommends, ask employees about their best experiences with the change at hand, collect their ideas of what success looks like, and gather suggestions on how this might be actualized.

5. **Create a culture of caring**

Finally, and perhaps most importantly, create a culture of caring. What is the biggest drain on resilience at work? A *Harvard Business Review* article reported that 75 percent of the British employees surveyed feel the biggest workplace drain is not the speed of change but managing difficult workplace relationships and politics.

Similarly, research by Dr. Rebecca Erickson demonstrates that the emotional context of the workplace correlates with burnout. Employees working in environments with low trust and high levels of agitation, frustration, and futility report stress levels and burnout rates nearly three times higher than employees who work in positive emotional environments. Positive, stable emotional work environments serve as an inoculation against burnout caused by workplace stress.

To foster change resilience, create a space where it is safe to voice opinions, share ideas, and make mistakes. Practically speaking, one of the most powerful things you can do for your team is create personal connections and a psychologically safe work environment. A culture of caring that says, "We are in this together," strengthens change resilience in yourself and among others. Ask the magic question: "What do you need and how can I help?" Become intentional about investing in relationships with your coworkers.

6. **Taking action**

The speed of change continues to accelerate, but it is the quality of change leadership that drains or sustains. By employing the aforementioned five strategies, leaders can foster the ability to bounce back from change quickly, implement change readily, and sustain ongoing resilience continually.

Building a resilient workforce will provide the organization with the tools needed to move forward in today's changing landscape. This will not only increase organization's readiness for change and productivity but will also increase innovation and creativity as well.

Leaders of resilient organizations do not allow their employees to get distracted by the stress or tension in times of change. They realistically acknowledge the challenging conditions, learn from mistakes, and find creative ways to overcome. Resilient leaders know that success in business is never assured and failure is never final.

Grit

Perlis (2013) notes that grit, in the context of behavior, is defined as "firmness of character; indomitable spirit." Duckworth, based on her studies, tweaked this definition to be "perseverance and passion for long-term goals."

Perlis states that while a key component of grit is resilience, resilience is the powering mechanism that draws your head up, moves you forward, and helps you persevere despite whatever obstacles you face along the way.

Duckworth (2016) also notes: "Grit is having stamina," she continues. "Grit is sticking with your future, day in, day out, not just for the week, not just for the month, but for years, and working really hard to make that future a reality."

Grit is important because it is a driver of achievement and success, independent of and beyond what talent and intelligence contribute. Being naturally smart and talented are great, but to truly do well and thrive, we need the ability to persevere. Without grit, talent may be nothing more than unmet potential. It is only with effort that talent becomes a skill that leads to success (Duckworth 2016).

She offers five common characteristics of grit:

1. **Courage**

   When you think of courage, you may think of physical bravery, but there are many other forms of courage. After all, courage is not the absence of fear but the triumph over it. Examples of courage include taking a chance when others will not; following your vision, no matter where it takes you; standing up for what you believe in, especially when your beliefs are unpopular; or simply doing the right thing even though easier options exist. The qualities of courageous people include patience, the ability to believe the unbelievable, and the guts to say "no." They are not afraid of taking an unpopular stand, nor of asking for help. They are able to forgive and move on quickly but also to stay the course when everyone else has abandoned ship.

2. **Conscientiousness**

   Conscientiousness is defined as the personality trait of being thorough, careful, or vigilant. Conscientiousness implies a desire to do a task well and conscientious people are efficient and organized, not resting until the job is done and done right. Generally, the conscientious have strong moral principles and values: they want to do the right thing and opinions and beliefs on any subject are rarely held lightly. They also tend to be perfectionists who like to do everything "the right way." In addition, the conscientious person is dedicated to work and is capable of intense, single-minded effort. They like the appearance of orderliness and tidiness and are good organizers, catalogers, and list makers. Finally, conscientious people stick to their convictions and opinions—opposition only serves to strengthen their dogged determination.

3. **Perseverance**

   "If you are going through hell, keep going," Winston Churchill famously said. Indeed, to many people, perseverance is synonymous with pain and suffering but those with true grit are able to flip their perspective on perseverance 180 degrees and view struggle as a doorway to pleasure. Essentially, to persevere means to start and continue steadfastly on the path toward any goal you set and frequently this factor alone is the difference between failure and success. However, one of the distinctions between someone who succeeds and someone who is just spending a lot of time doing something is this: practice must have purpose. That's where long-term goals come in. They provide the context and framework in which to find the meaning and value of your long-term efforts, which helps cultivate drive, sustainability, passion, courage, stamina, and grit.

4. **Resilience**

In one word, resilience is "toughness"—the capacity to recover quickly from difficulties. In general, those who are extremely optimistic tend to show greater resilience. They approach life with a sense of humor, are able to laugh at themselves, and to reframe situations and experiences to see a lighter side. Resilient people also tend to have a strong moral compass or set of beliefs that cannot be shattered. They don't compare themselves to others, knowing instead that they are their own yardstick of success. They also see difficulties as stepping stones to transformation. Finally, they do not try to control their lives. Instead, they cultivate self-awareness and practice mindfulness. They surrender themselves to life's ups and downs and adjust their attitudes and goals according to the size of the wave they are currently riding.

5. **Passion**

Passion creates excellence when mediocrity will do. Passionate people have a deep sense of purpose and are often selfless in their actions. They also know themselves—they have a clear sense of their values and beliefs, and they live by them. They generally accept themselves as imperfect and growing, seeing life as a series of choices and options. They are driven by goals and are result-oriented. They don't let anything stop them—they have a "will to find a way" attitude and don't accept "no" for an answer. By the same token, they are also enthusiastic about the success of others. Finally, they take responsibility for their lives but are not afraid to ask for support. Passionate people recognize that they are in the driver's seat as they travel on their journey of life.

Grit is "sticktoitiveness"; a diligent spirit; the nagging conviction that keeps you pressing on when it'd be easier to give up. Grit is what makes you get back on the horse after you've been kicked off. Grit is the realization that achieving one's greatest potential comes from running a marathon, not a sprint.

Clear (n.d.) noted that mentally tough leaders are more consistent than their peers. They have a clear goal that they work toward each day. They don't let short-term profits, negative feedback, or hectic schedules prevent them from continuing the march toward their vision. They make a habit of building up the people around them—not just once, but over and over and over again.

Reframing Resistance

Murphy (2016) notes: "the key to successful change management is getting people to let go of the status quo and reach for something bigger and better."

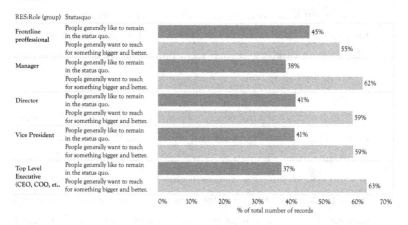

Given how infrequently employees are asked to participate in originating a change effort, it makes sense that they would evidence more pessimism about leaving the status quo than top executives. As is in most cases of good leadership, transparency and inclusion in big changes help abate much of the anxiety and concerns that come with change. In today's world, work and life are considered heavily connected. As such, the insecurity that comes with change affects employees personally in greater ways than ever before. Smoothing out these anxieties in a planful way will position a leader for success.

If you're going to persuade employees to leave the status quo and reach for something bigger, you need to clearly explain three things: why this change is necessary, where this change will take us, and how we're going to get from here to there. The "why" creates a need and urgency for change and stops people from eulogizing the past ("the way we used to do it was so much better"). The "where" provides positive forward direction that turns the anxiety of "why" into excitement. And the "how" gets people comfortable with the idea that they can be successful.

Alsher (2015) offered these five "truths" about resistance to change:

Truth #1: Even when you are making a "positive change," you will encounter resistance.

The fact that you are dealing with a "positive change" has nothing to do with the levels of resistance you will encounter. Instead, the level of resistance is directly linked to the level of disruption created by the change. Not from your Frame of Reference (FOR) but from the FOR of the individual Targets. Remember, FORs are different! What's "positive" to one group is not necessarily positive for another. The ongoing challenge is to understand all the FORs affected by the change.

Truth #2: The greatest resistance to change is usually in the middle to upper levels of management, not from the "front lines" of the change.

Often, one of the biggest shocks to our clients is that resistance to a transformational change will be greatest in the middle to upper layers of their organization, not at the front lines of the change. While at first glance this is surprising, we have yet to find clients who don't agree this is the case in their own organizations. The *AIM* (*Accelerating Implementation Methodology*) principle says, "you can expect the highest level of resistance from those people with the greatest interest in things remaining the same." Who are these people? They're the mid- to high-level management personnel. Why are they resisting? Because it's often these individuals that have the most to "lose" in terms of power and prestige.

Truth #3: Resistance to change is cumulative

The frustrating truth is that the resistance you encounter today may be due to a change that failed several years ago. In fact, you can find that you are still dealing with resistance years after a project is supposedly complete! Whether leaders recognize it or not, your organization is always learning lessons. For example, the lesson may be "If I resist this change and continue to do my job as I have always done it, this change will go away, too." The truth is poorly managed implementations often have a long-term, residual impact.

Truth #4: Communication alone will not eliminate resistance

The assumption is that if we just tell people about the change, and tell them more often, we will eliminate resistance. But the truth of the matter is you will never eliminate resistance by piling on logical and rational explanations for why the change will be good for people. A sound change management methodology like the *Accelerating Implementation Methodology* (*AIM*) certainly includes communication planning, but if you take a look at the *AIM* roadmap, you will see that communication is only one of the 10 elements for managing organizational changes! Bottom-line: A Communication Plan is not an Implementation Plan!

Truth #5: You will never be able to eliminate resistance. Instead, you need to manage it.

You will never combat or overcome resistance to change. Sure, it's frustrating, especially when you think your change will make things better for the people who are affected by it. But if you are looking to drive innovation or transformation into your organization, you should anticipate upfront that you are going to create high levels of disruption and consequently high levels of resistance to change.

Heathfield (2021b) stated resistance to change is the unwillingness to adapt to altered circumstances. It can be covert or overt, organized, or individual. Employees may realize they don't like or want a change and resist publicly, and that can be very disruptive. Employees can also feel uncomfortable with the changes introduced and resist, sometimes unknowingly, through their actions, their language, and in the stories and conversations they share in the workplace.

As discussed in the previous chapters, in our current day, such publicly shared dissatisfaction will spread quickly and harm both the process and potentially the organization, whether deserved or not. With employee acquisition and retention both becoming and ever-increasing arms race, such dissatisfaction should be addressed quickly and preemptively whenever possible.

In a worst-case scenario, employees can be forceful in their refusal to adopt any changes, bringing confrontation and conflict to your organization.

Resistance to change is evident in actions such as:

- Criticism
- Nitpicking
- Snide comments or sarcastic remarks
- Missed meetings
- Failed commitments
- Endless arguments
- Sabotage

Barriers to organizational change

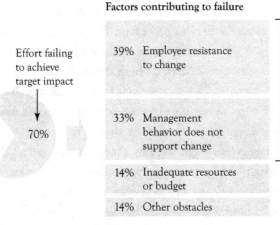

Factors contributing to failure

Effort failing to achieve target impact

70%

39% Employee resistance to change

33% Management behavior does not support change

14% Inadequate resources or budget

14% Other obstacles

Health-related factors

Source: www.pinterest.com/pin/1407443609558340/

Heathfield (2021b) states when employees are poorly introduced to changes that affect how they work, especially when they don't see the need for the changes, they may be resistant. They may also experience resistance when they haven't been involved in the decision-making process.

Resistance to change can intensify if employees feel they have been involved in a series of changes that have had insufficient support to gain the anticipated results. They also become weary when changes happen too frequently, becoming a flavor-of-the-month instead of strategic action.

Organizations are constantly evolving, which means change is inevitable. But introducing changes without consulting the people they affect, explaining the need for change, and providing support through the process will alienate your employees and drag down morale.

When a change is introduced in this environment, with a lot of discussions and employee involvement, resistance to change is minimized. Resistance is also minimized if there is a widespread belief that the changes are needed and will have a positive effect.

Nobl (n.d.) states that organizational and cultural change succeeds when:

- *Change is safe to try.* When someone feels threatened, they are far less likely to take risks and change how they work. Our process creates environments where change is "safe to try" both to bolster individual courage and to ensure no single change can risk harm to your overall business.
- *Change is cocreated.* People are far more willing to embrace change when they have had a hand in deciding and shaping the change itself. Our process invites your teams to ideate and respond to the changes required for your market.
- *Change becomes a habit.* It's both cliché and accurate to say that change is the new normal for most industries. We train your teams to continually sense external forces and mount internal change programs long after we're gone.
- *Change acknowledges loss.* Any change, even when it's clearly the right change to make, triggers feelings of loss: loss of pride; loss of control; loss of narrative; loss of competence; loss of time; loss of familiarity. Our change process includes key moments to recognize and address those feelings of loss.

Tams, (2018) argue that the flaws of the traditional change management model are themselves a symptom of a larger problem. Many organizations are simply not set up for agile change. While managers are busy relentlessly communicating about the change imperative, the design of many organizations slants the playing field toward controllability, stability, routinization, risk-avoidance, zero-tolerance for error, or deference to authority. It's like pushing the accelerator and the brakes at the same time. The result is friction, fatigue, and cynicism. If we push change onto an organization that is built for stability, nothing good will come of it. Pushing harder won't do the trick. If, instead, we get the organization ready for change, we must worry about resistance much less.

Alsher (2015) notes that resistance is not all bad. It's a natural part of the change process and can actually be a sign of organizational health! A good change agent will take advantage of resistance and use it as project feedback. If it is purposefully managed, resistance can increase communication, promote genuine involvement, build resiliency, and create opportunity for buy in to occur.

CHAPTER 9

The C⁶ Change Leadership Framework

In revisiting our original research (2006), which revealed the presence of Change Fatigue™, we conducted additional research into the literature and practices around change management. We also deployed our original Change Management Framework (the "C⁵" framework) in two test cases. We learned from the additional research and the two test cases that we needed to add another element, *conversion*.

It is proposed that this updated change leadership framework, the "C⁶" framework, developed largely from the lessons learned from the adaptive enterprise, be deployed as a means to lead organizational change in a manner than sustains and embeds change as a natural practice of the firm's day-to-day activities. And to make change a natural process and part of the firm's DNA.

Leaders need to be "ambassadors for change."

Future leaders may be humble—but they still need to be visible. From Apple's Tim Cook to Starbucks' Howard Schultz, top CEOs are more than simply chief decision-makers.

They're also brand ambassadors who, having created a strong company culture, champion that culture in the world at large. And as the business world becomes more competitive, it's these figures who will empower staff through leading by example (B-Team 2015).

The C⁶ framework is developed around six leadership competencies: communications, collaboration, confidence, cohesion, climate, and conversion (see Figure 9.1). The change from the C⁵ version to the C⁶ version was the addition of the "conversion" element.

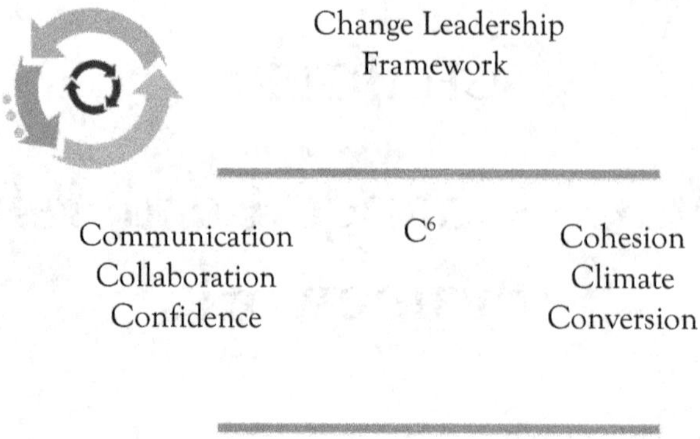

Change Leadership
Framework

Communication	C^6	Cohesion
Collaboration		Climate
Confidence		Conversion

Figure 9.1 C^6 Change Management Framework

Communication

Leaders today must be able to create a compelling change vision, communicate it effectively to drive buy-in across and down the organization, and then lead its execution to reach the expected outcomes. The key to the success of any executive is the ability to communicate effectively. Can you imagine an effective leader who is not an effective communicator? Leading change is a communication-intensive process. It demands leaders consistently and persistently communicate using every available communication medium. When employees are on board and engaged with the change initiative, the chances of launching a successful change strategy increases by 30 percent (smarp 2021).

The leader is often the catalyst for change. A leader today must inspire and convince constituents that change is necessary, get others to buy-in, reassures, and follows the change through to embed it into the DNA of the organization. Being an effective change agent as a leader has become a critical leadership competency for 21st century leaders.

As many as 73 percent of change-affected employees report experiencing moderate to high stress levels. Those suffering from change-related stress perform 5 percent worse than the average employee (smarp 2021).

A Towers Watson study found that while 68 percent of senior managers say they understand why organizational change is happening, the number falls from there. Only 53 percent of middle managers really get the message, and only 40 percent of front-line supervisors understand the change (smarp 2021).

McKinsey & Company found that organizations where the senior leadership communicated openly throughout the organization about change progress were 8× more likely to succeed than those who did not (Kelley 2016).

You cannot overcommunicate when you are asking your organization to change. Every successful senior manager who has led a successful change management effort expresses the need for overcommunicating during a change experience and makes this statement in retrospect (Heathfield 2021a).

There are some basics here that some leaders seem to forget:

- Communicate consistently, frequently, and through multiple channels, including speaking, writing, video, training, focus groups, bulletin boards, intranets, and more about the change.
- Communicate all that is known about the changes, as quickly as the information is available. Make clear that your bias is toward instant communication, so some of the details may change at a later date. Tell people that your other choice is to hold all communication until you are positive about the decisions, goals, and progress, which is disastrous in effective change management.
- Provide significant amounts of time for people to ask questions, request clarification, and provide input. If you've ever been part of a scenario in which a leader presented changes to a large group via overhead transparencies and then fled, you know what bad news this is for change integration. People must feel involved in the change. Involvement creates commitment—nothing else is as significant during a change process.
- Clearly communicate the vision, mission, and objectives of the change management effort. Help people to understand how these changes will affect them personally. If you don't help with this process, people will make up their own stories, usually more negative than the truth.

- Recognize that true communication is a conversation. It is two-way, and real discussion must result. It cannot be just a presentation.
- The change leaders or sponsors need to spend time conversing one-on-one or in small groups with the people who are expected to make the changes.
- Communicate the reasons for the changes in such a way that people understand the context, the purpose, and the need. Practitioners have called this "building a memorable, conceptual framework" and "creating a theoretical framework to underpin the change."
- Provide answers to questions only if you know the answer. Leaders destroy their credibility when they provide incorrect information or appear to stumble or back-peddle when providing an answer. It is much better to say you don't know and that you will try to find out.
- Communication should be proactive. If the rumor mill is already in action, the organization has waited too long to communicate (Healthfield 2021a).

The first element, *communications*, is of primary importance in reframing change. Leaders have learned that the effective flow of timely information serves to fuel adaptability. If employees understand the context, relationships, strategy, and tactical needs, they are better prepared to adapt to changes in the environment on a real or near real-time basis. Employees need to understand the explicit reasons for change, the expected outcomes, and the performance expectations. Improved and timely information will go a long way to increasing the employee's capacity for change. "Sharing data and information in a transparent manner will ensure that everyone is in the loop, and that everyone is aware of any potential issues with the business, product or service that can be addressed in a collaborative manner" (Johnson 2020). Wanberg and Banas (2000) found that during change, the timely exchange of information increased employee's openness to change. Nelson and Cooper (1995) found that during times of uncertainty (change), a "climate of secrecy" and a lack of communication leads to poor morale and job dissatisfaction (p. 65). Sharing data and information in a transparent manner will ensure that everyone is in the loop, and that everyone is aware of any potential issues with the business, product, or service that can be addressed in a collaborative manner" (Johnson 2020).

In order to use communication skills to speed up change acceptance, leaders should utilize a staged approach to the communication process: first, gain others' attention; second, establish awareness and understanding. Leaders can then do the third: gain the advantage of persuading others (Mai and Ankerson 2003).

Dunford, Palmer, and Akin (2009) argue that leaders must use a broader array of communication skills to drive change including more listening, the creation of active, bidirectional feedback mechanisms, the use of stories, and doing more "selling." Leaders can effectively "sell" the needed adaptations by linking the change vision to the business impacts, continuously and consistently communicating the change story and by focusing on incremental changes so the scale does not distract the workforce. They go on to say that talking in stages, talking coherently, and creating a common change language are critical to effective change communication.

One of the main tasks of a facilitator can be compared with an orchestra conductor, cuing members and "guiding the use of their instruments toward the desired result" (Cserti 2019).

Unsuccessful leaders tended to focus on the "what" behind the change. Successful leaders communicated the "what" *and* the "why." Leaders who explained the purpose of the change and connected it to the organization's values or explained the benefits created stronger buy-in and urgency for the change (The Center for Creative Leadership n.d.).

There are four stages of change communication (smarp 2021).

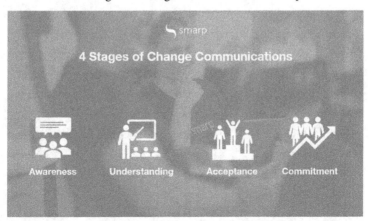

1. *Awareness*: Building internal awareness through clear, timely, and personalized change communication sent via employees' favorite communication channels in order to eliminate or mitigate employees' fear and resistance to change.

2. *Understanding*: Communicating the what, why, how, when, who as well as the WIIFM (what's in it for me) is important to help employees understand the benefits of the change and see the positive sides of it.

3. *Acceptance*: In this stage, employees accept the change and act in accordance with their employer's instructions. However, it is the employer's job to keep employees updated, encourage their share of voice, and make them feel involved in the process.

4. *Commitment*: Once employees accept change, change communication is not done. Moreover, this is the stage in which most change initiatives fail. Communication needs to keep flowing, employees need to be able to collaborate, and employers need to spot and reward their change ambassadors (smarp, 2021).

Devries (2017) offers some ideas on the mistakes to avoid when communicating change.

Mistake 1: Many well-meaning managers attempt to improve change communications by going the direct route.

These managers naturally want to talk directly to employees, usually supported by the advice of senior human resources staff or consultants. Unfortunately, it is a mistake that is wrong for two reasons.

First, it can be viewed as a mere symbolic move, and today's disillusioned employee has little love for the empty gesture. Second, and more damaging, these campaigns can weaken the relationship between workers and their team leaders. Team members want to work for someone who is connected and has a degree of power within the organization. They want to know their supervisor has some pull, and is not viewed as powerless.

Mistake 2: Other well-intentioned leaders push for equality in the workplace.

They believe leaders should sit shoulder-to-shoulder with employees to hear the big news.

Again, a mistaken strategy because it is evidence of management's failure to recognize the team leader's superior status. This reduces the person's perceived power and weakens his or her effectiveness as a force of change. What many leaders fail to realize is that the only communications with the power to change behavior is the kind between a team leader and a team member.

Mistake 3: Applying the strategy that more must be better, executives in charge of change campaigns use ink by the barrel.

They think the solution is more employee reports, posters, news bulletins, video scripts, team briefing outlines, brochures, and guidebooks. This too is the wrong approach, because the critical communication is the type that happens face-to-face.

Energy and resources should be directed toward producing briefing cards that will arm leaders to answer the key questions that are in the minds of staff members.

Mistake 4: Not giving team leaders a persuasive story to tell can be a tactical error.

Storytelling helps persuade at an emotional level. Stories are the building blocks of an organization's culture.

If there is already a true story to tell about how the change will benefit the organization and its employees, so much the better. If not, at least give people a narrative to tell about how success can be achieved in the future. Every story starts with the name of a character who wants something. Make your main character likable or the victim of undeserved misfortune so the listeners will root for them. To make the individual likable, describe some of their good qualities or attributes.

Heroes need help on their journey. They need to work with a wise person. This is where your organization comes in. Be the voice of wisdom and experience. The hero does not succeed alone; they succeed because of the help you provided.

Also give the listeners the moral of the story. Take a cue from Aesop, the man who gave us fables like *The Tortoise and the Hare* (the moral: slow and steady wins the race). Don't count on the listeners to get the message. The storyteller's final job is to tell them what the story means.

To recap this "C"—Sibbett and Wendling (2018) note the need to hear all voices and for leaders to create a consistent environment of dialogue. Dialogue is the practice of leveraging the power of the whole to receptively listen to diverse perspectives, suspend judgments, and explore assumptions. This can help transform thinking into assumptions and potentially wisdom by appreciating complexity and allowing creative tensions to forge new solutions.

They offer these "dialogic practices":

- Working with intention
- Supporting readiness to share and explore
- Creating safety and nonjudgment
- Making group agreements
- Listening deeply
- Asking generative questions
- Normalizing ambiguity
- Facilitating pivotal conversations and reach exchange
- Holding the process open for emergence
- Avoiding premature closure
- Shifting from divergent to convergent exchange
- Tracking collective insights

It seems clear from both research and experience that timely and open communications is an essential element in reducing stress and improving job satisfaction. Gibson, O'Leary, and Weintraub (2020) stress the importance of frequent and clear communication in order to ensure that employees know their value to the organization.

Collaboration

For future business, collaboration will be a key driver to success. In an article for *The Guardian*, Neville Isdell and Clare Melford point out that as the world changes, "new collaborations will emerge between governments, businesses and not-for-profit organizations" (B-Team 2015).

Leaders need to be connectors adept on connecting an array of stakeholders and in creating relationships that can be leveraged to achieve the change vision of an organization. Collaborative connector behavior includes silo-busting, building trust, aligning body language, promoting diversity, sharpening soft skills, and creating psychological safety. (Goman 2017).

Kelley (2016) also noted the critical need for the "C-suite" executives leading change to connect with a "network of change agents." He refers to the need for senior executives to connect with key influential employees across and down the organization. These are "forward thinking" individuals who can help drive change ownership as well as successful implementation of change initiatives.

Making meaningful and sustainable change requires collaboration and strong leadership. While not as evident a value to some, collaboration is essential to change efforts and results. Change cannot happen if leaders and functions within the organization operate autonomously and are siloed off. One of the first steps in change management will be a shift in the culture to a more collaborative organization, across units, across geographic boundaries, and among functions, roles, and status levels (Cross, 2021).

Valdellon (2017) offered the following benefits are realized by businesses that have a collaborative culture:

1. More flexibility as an organization, enhanced ability to manage sudden change
2. More engaged employees through teamwork and camaraderie
3. Healthier employees
4. Higher retention rates of employees
5. Enhanced ability to attract top talent
6. More productive meetings
7. Accelerated production and creation of value
8. Innovation is spurred
9. Better alignment with stakeholders, especially with clients
10. Better individual productivity
11. Increased profitability

This element, *collaboration*, is also very important to the concept of "adapt and survive" (Capgemini 2003, 8). The pace and complexity of the current environment exposes weak links in organizations. It is not realistic to expect organizations or employees to be able to thrive in this environment by going it alone. Change risks pulling an organization apart: trust weakens, silos or impenetrable bunkers develop as people cling onto their jobs and seek to strengthen their power bases. People can become wary, feel isolated, and uncertain; creativity and productivity can take a dive (Macaulay n.d.).

Collaboration is the act of people working together to reach a common goal. Collaboration is the way that all the people in an enterprise function together. Better collaboration means better operations. With improved collaboration, organizations can increase the scale and capacity of their processes and develop new ways of doing business (Cisco 2011).

The need for collaboration with suppliers, customers, and other stakeholders is essential for the organization to seize opportunities or to thwart threats. It is equally unrealistic to expect employees to meet the challenges they face day to day by themselves. The growth of the use of teams in organizations is evidence of the need to find ways to leverage current assets to create new responses. Collaboration is fueled at the employee level through the timely exchange of information and meaningful participation in the analysis and implementation processes. Involving employees early in the process improves engagement and broadens the scope of relevant exchanges between management and employees. Leaders have learned that involving employees in tactical discussions can improve unit performance and adaptability without undermining the chain of command. The goal of a collaborative process is to ensure a holistic perspective is developed. This will likely lead to fewer surprises and more integrated responses. Research indicates that change initiatives have a higher level of success when there is clear communication about the change initiative, an opportunity for participation in the process and a shared interest in its success (Daniels and Hollifield 2002).

Newton (2017) offered these insights to link collaboration and change.

It takes more than informing and updating other business leaders on our change-initiative developments. To drive collaborative change:

- *Before looking forward, look around.* Rather than putting all initial energy into planning how the initiative will be successfully achieved, first investigate what other changes are going on across the business and explore what they really mean. We need to go beyond surface understanding of others' change initiatives and consider how we might be able to work together to unearth potentially overlooked mutual gains.

- *Put your hand up to drive collaboration in practice.* It's easy to talk about collaborating across the business, but in reality, change-silos often form because nobody has clear responsibility for bringing the different change leaders of the various initiatives together. Volunteer to host regular "change hubs" where leaders driving change across the business can gather to share updates and identify overlaps, mutual challenges, and collaborative gains.

- *Focus on reducing uncertainty and building trust.* Certainty is one of the key components of collaborating with others. We are often reluctant to collaborate in practice because we are uncertain about the reality of others' work. Seek to better understand colleagues' work; in doing so, you increase your trust in their expertise, and their trust in yours.

- *Carve out time for deeper conversations.* Out habit and busyness, we often jump quickly from small talk to detailed agenda points in meetings. In doing so, we skip over the conversations that would help us better understand the bigger picture of our colleagues' work. Start meetings with a couple of open questions to understand colleagues' broader priorities, current opportunities, and challenges.

- *Bring your external consultants together.* As an external consultant, I've experienced times when the client has encouraged us to work together with other advisers brought in for their different expertise. I've also experienced times when I've been aware that other consultants are working in different but (at least to my mind) related areas of the business and we have been kept almost intentionally separate from them. Where

any external advisers are brought in for projects, there are
more gains than losses in bringing them together to share and
drive collaboration across the business.

When change leaders across the business collaborate and coordinate, we position ourselves to bring greater clarity, lead more effectively, and drive changes more successfully. Successful change leaders aim for whole-hearted engagement with the change and commitment to making it work.

To help ensure any change you lead is sustained, identify early on those people within your organization who exert influence, at whatever level they operate. These people may not always have the title manager or leader, but they will be influencers and leaders in their own way. They will be essential to get on side if you want to foster a sense of shared ownership throughout your organization. Encourage teamwork and collaboration throughout the change process.

Collaborative leadership across an organization is an essential ingredient to making change stick. To be effective, organizations must develop a network of leaders throughout their organization willing and able to demonstrate true collaboration, involvement, and teamwork (Macaulay n.d.).

Confidence

The next element, *confidence*, serves to build employee resiliency. Leaders must adopt an attitude of confidence in order to help manage employee stress during times of change. Wanberg and Banas (2000) found that optimism and perceived control were associated with openness to change. Jimmieson, Terry, and Callan (2004) note that the employees perceived ability to function has a moderating effect on job stress. In other words, if the employee has confidence about his/her ability to perform (self-efficacy), the debilitating effects of stress are reduced. Change-related confidence is an important buffer against workplace stressors (Wanberg and Banas 2000). An employee with a high level of self-efficacy is confident of "dealing with unexpected events, stays calm in the midst of difficulties and is able to handle whatever comes his or her way" (Tiong 2005, 30). Confidence also comes with experience. Lau, Tse, and Zhou (2002) note that people with more change experiences and more freedom to change will have a more positive outlook on about change. A positive change outlook leads to reduced stress and improved change openness.

It starts with both the organization's and individual's readiness for change. Smith (2015) noted that readiness is made up of:

- Employees' collective desire for the change;
- Employees' belief that the change is possible/not too risky; and
- The ability of existing systems within the business to accommodate the change.

Dym and Hutson (n.d.) noted several points about the role of "readiness" for change:

Readiness is derived from the Greek word, "arariskein," which means "fitting" or "joining" or "being arranged for use." So it is that certain kinds of interventions fit best in particular organizational climates at particular times—and not in others. A system can be entered at any point, because all of its elements are interconnected. This is the nub of it—when interactions are aligned according to both timing and fit, there is readiness.

Readiness takes many forms. Sometimes, people and organizations are in so much pain that they believe they must change. At other times, systems are so out of kilter, so uncertain or disorganized, that they can't help but change in their efforts to regain their balance. At still other times, people are so open, curious, and receptive to the influence of a new leader that they see every new idea or program as pointing the path to successful action. There is much variety but the core principle seems clear: Organizations change when they are ready.

When ready, they will pick up almost anything from the environment and make use of it. Even the slightest nudge from a manager can act as a powerful catalyst. Conversely, when people are not ready to change, they will ignore or resist the best efforts of others to change them. As anyone who has repeatedly tried to act less defensively or more assertively knows, we resist even our own plans to change.

They go further by noting:

Leading organizational change theorists, such as Marvin Weisbord, Ronald Heifetz, and of course Kurt Lewin, recognize the importance of readiness. Each, in a different way, has advocated the location of change efforts outside the stable center of organizations and the encouragement of creative processes that thrive when people and ideas interact freely and in unfamiliar ways, before solid plans and strategies are formulated.

One of the keys to developing confidence is to increase readiness to change. This can start with recognizing what Dym and Hutsion (n.d.) called "forays."

No matter how rigidly or bureaucratically organized systems are or may appear, there are always changes afoot—people are constantly trying to improve things. Leaders and other change agents must learn to see these forays for what they are: tentative, incomplete moves that people and organizations make to improve their organization. Their efforts are forays from one way of doing or thinking about things into another.

Forays are present in all organizations, all of the time. It is essential for leaders to learn to spot them. If we can identify and support forays to help them grow and use the momentum of people's own energies, then we have access to the most powerful change agent possible.

Many leaders plan and implement change efforts with hardly a thought to the readiness of their employees. They may assume that persuasion and reason will win the day. Or rather than picking their moments, leaders may try to create a permanent state of readiness for change in a negative way, by declaring that "only the paranoid survive," or in a positive way, by striving to create a "learning organization."

An investment in training and preparation is also seen as a means to improve confidence. The idea is to build muscle memory (change memory) that allows for fast response as conditions demand. The constant focus on preparation also builds confidence in the firm's ability to adapt. Combined with appropriate information flow, preparation expands the perspectives and confidence of the unit members. The more informed and prepared employees are, the more resilient and adaptable they become.

To build confidence, leaders need to develop the readiness to change and also to increase resilience.

One way to assess readiness to change, keeping the change vision in mind, is to create a frame using a "start, stop, continue" assessment (Kelley 2016) using these three questions:

1. What behaviors and beliefs will the individuals and the organization need to have (start)?
2. What behaviors and beliefs will the individuals and the organization need to stop?
3. What behaviors and beliefs will the individuals and the organization continue to have?

This may seem like a fairly simple assessment, but the purpose is a bit more complex assessment. Ideally, the leadership team (and other key stakeholders) use this process to focus on both the current and future state at the same time. The participants have to decide what to carry forward, what to abandon, and what new processes may be needed.

Ovans (2015) note that resilience refers to a person's capacity to handle difficulties, demands, and high pressure without becoming stressed. This is manifested in four ways: *the ability to "not sweat the small stuff."* They maintain their good cheer despite the frustrations and hassles that are part of everyday work life. *The ability to perform well under pressure.* Resilient people handle pressure well. *The ability to respond flexibly and adapt to changing circumstances.* Resilient people respond resourcefully to change. Rather than fight change and hang on to old, outdated ways, they respond to change with confidence and flexibility. *The ability to bounce back from defeat and disaster.* The more resilient a person is, the more quickly they are able to recover from a setback, make the best of the new situation. The more resilient a workforce, the more it can handle heavy workloads, pressures, and major changes with less stress.

Coutu (2002) said this about resilience:

Resilient people possess three characteristics—a staunch acceptance of reality; a deep belief, often buttressed by strongly held values, that life is meaningful; and an uncanny ability to improvise. You can bounce back from hardship with just one or two of these qualities, but you will only be truly resilient with all three. These three characteristics hold true for resilient organizations as well....Resilient people and companies face reality with staunchness, make meaning of hardship instead of crying out in despair, and improvise solutions from thin air. Others do not.

Proctor (2020) added:

The real value of resilience for organizations lies in the ability to successfully implement business imperatives. Most change projects fail because the people involved are just not resilient enough to deal with the perpetual change loading—where change projects continue to be undertaken without any assessment of whether the change capacity exists to deliver them successfully in the organization.

Resilience is the quality that enables one person to bounce back, actually respond well, and thrive with multiple challenges, while a colleague, with apparently similar skills and experience, struggles to cope.

She adds that these are seven key characteristics of resilient people:

1. Optimistic: Resilient people believe that change will have a positive outlook. They are able to analyze even an apparently dire situation in a way that gives them hope for the future.
2. Self-assured: Resilient people have a strong but realistic belief in their own capabilities. As a result, they tend to control change, rather than the change controlling them.

3. Focused: Resilient people have the focus needed to be able to prioritize activities effectively. They can pursue goals successfully, even in the face of adversity.

4. Open to ideas: Resilient people have an open mind to different tactics and strategies. They tend to be good at generating alternative approaches and solutions to match the changing situation.

5. Seek support: Resilient people actively seek the support of others during times of change. They look for opportunities to involve the skills and experience of other people as well as their own.

6. Structured: Resilient people are able to analyze the situation and create an effective plan to implement change, with enough flexibility built in to cope with the shifting situation.

7. Proactive: Resilient people are prepared to step out into the "unknown" and take the action necessary to make change.

Increasing confidence is essential to creating a sustained focus on productive change. It starts by accessing and increasing change readiness and then building resilience through change experiences.

Cohesion

In today's fast-paced, ever-changing business environment, driving deeper levels of cohesion can mean the difference between success and failure. Primarily because cooperation and unity and the related social connections can create collective confidence during change periods.

Cohesion is all about organizational identification. A high level of organizational cohesion improves morale and communication, builds resiliency, and improves adaptability. Members of the organization take pride in membership and form strong bonds with their peers. Members can identify with a shared mission, vision, and values to align their personal interests, harness their collective expertise, and focus their individual efforts.

Puusa and Tolvanen (2006) note that organization identity, when realized by organization members, has an effect on how strongly individuals within the organization identify themselves with the organization. Therefore, a strong identification results in the level of trust and in that way creates stronger commitment to the organization and its goals. Resilience refers to the ability to cope with ongoing disruptive change, bounce back easily from setbacks, overcome adversities, change to a new way of working and living when an old way is no longer possible, and do all this without acting in a dysfunctional or harmful manner. Leaders must lead in a constantly changing world. Some staff make it difficult by resisting or fighting the ongoing changes. Others adapt and flow with them. Leaders who understand the importance of workforce resiliency can help employees navigate through rough periods of change skillfully and easily (Siebert 2005).

Van Dick, Wagner, and Lemmer (2004) note that organizational identity serves to describe what organizational members think is central to the organization, what distinguishes the organization from others, and what the members perceive to be enduring about the organization. Membership in the organization and peer relationships provides an enduring sense of belonging despite the organizational changes that may have occurred. Organizational identity is positively associated with employee attitudes during times of change. A positive organizational identity is also positively correlated with job satisfaction (Van Dick, Wagner, and Lemmer 2004). Additionally, social support from leaders and colleagues has been shown to reduce stress and anxiety. Employees with positive work relationships have shown higher levels of motivation, unit loyalty, adaptability, and personal well-being (Tiong 2005).

Cohesiveness can be a positive factor while an organization is moving toward change. If you can get influential members of an organization to come together, you may also be able to get the outlying folks to come on board for reasons outlined in the aforementioned forces and actions that create and maintain cohesiveness. For example, Schultz, Sjøvold, and André (2017) noted that the nonparticipating group could still have a strong attraction to the others in the organization, they may be resistant to separating from those other members, or they may just be motivated to remain a member of the group. That connectedness and cohesiveness can drive change.

When cohesion is driven from leadership and is infused throughout the entire organization, the change management process will likely have a more successful outcome. The leader facilitates the preparation, support, and help, their employees need to make the change management process thrive. When group cohesiveness is conducted appropriately by the right leader within an organization, each element of the change management process will have a better chance for positive impact. The overall outcome will likely be enhanced for the organization as it moves through impending change.

Indeed (2021) noted that cohesion is important for a number of reasons. These reasons include:

- Better communication among team members
- A heightened ability to achieve company objectives and goals
- A decreased need to micromanage a team, freeing up time for managers
- A positive work environment
- A decreased use of resources due to a team's effectiveness and efficiency
- Increased job satisfaction among employees who are part of a cohesive team

These attributes can serve as a positive source for driving identification, collective resilience, and readiness for change.

There are some indicators that can be used to judge the level of cohesiveness in the organization (Indeed 2021):

- *Quick conflict resolution*: A high level of cohesion doesn't mean that conflict never arises. However, strong cohesion allows conflict to be resolved effectively by ensuring all members are heard and feel safe sharing their perspectives and ideas. The more cohesion the better members are at conflict resolution and avoiding major disagreements that can cause less cohesive teams to fall apart.
- *A strong sense of "we"*: Individuals who are part of a cohesive organization are willing to set aside their individual wants and needs to support the larger "we" of the group. This ultimately allows employees to work better together because members share a common vision and are committed to working on behalf of the organization rather than themselves.

- *Personal accountability*: Members of a highly cohesive organizations hold themselves accountable for the work they are responsible for. They understand that underperforming or not meeting goals affects the entire organization and are willing to remain accountable to ensure they do not contribute to a less effective team. Members are willing to be honest about their efforts and speak up when they are unable to meet deadlines.

- *Organizational prioritization*: Cohesive units are better able to maintain their focus on their organization's larger objectives and are less likely to get distracted by competition or diverse points of view. Members are more likely to put the organization's needs first and keep their own agendas at bay to reach organizational goals.

- *A high level of trust*: Trust is a major component of effective organization and it is a leadership priority to establish a high level of trust among organization members.

The higher level of cohesion in an organization will likely enable the organization to both embed adaptability into the DNA of the organization and also to positively navigate the vagaries which accompany many change initiatives.

Climate

The next element, *climate*, refers to the overall organizational environment created by managers. Organizational climate is the way people experience the work environment.

A positive, forward-facing, adaptive climate is more likely to reduce the debilitating aspects of stress related to change. Heflo (n.d.) notes "climate" is people's perceptions and feelings about their work environment.

Many leaders confuse climate with culture, thinking the climate cannot be controlled because it is too big and engrained in the organization. Spector (2019) notes:

The terms climate and culture are often used interchangeably, but they are not the same concept. Climate is part of culture and reflects the sorts of behaviors that are encouraged and presumably engaged in within an organization. Culture is far more than encouraged behavior patterns. Culture includes artifacts (e.g., the sorts of clothes people wear), symbols (e.g., the company logo), technology (e.g., salespeople's use of tablets to ring up sales), and values (e.g., profitability). Although these aspects of culture might support the climate, they go beyond climate, and much of organizational culture might not link to climate.

Savvy leaders know the climate can, in fact, be improved and that making necessary changes will move employees from anxiety to confidence and from isolation to connection. Building a climate that facilitates productive emotional experiences allows employees to achieve greater collaboration and performance. Climate is important because employees are likely to engage in the behaviors that are encouraged. To a great extent, climate is encouraged by the sorts of issues and problems the company deals with.

An environment of open-communications fostering the meaningful exchange of timely and appropriate information will improve decision making and adaptability. An environment that appreciates initiative, prefers to learn versus blame, and promotes organizational membership will likely increase the resiliency of its members. Managers must learn not to overcontrol and to encourage employees to expect the unexpected. Managers cannot expect to make every decision or to manage all the daily stressors that employees face. Employees must be empowered to deal with as many situations that arise as possible. Empowerment improves adaptability. Tiong (2005) found that a high level of involvement in the process of change improved employee motivation and unit loyalty. Employees must learn to be flexible and to see change as a natural part of organizational life. Strong social support must be institutionalized into the organizational environment to help improve flexibility and adaptability. Finally, managers must create an environment that supports unit cohesion by promoting esprit-de-corps so that members take pride in membership.

Spector (2019) notes that climates are built through both actions and messaging. He suggests some steps to build organizational climate:

- Climate is a strategic decision. Top management should decide what is important and what should be emphasized. Climate often means trade-offs because resources devoted to one thing are not available for another. Safety, for example, requires effort and time. Is it okay to take five minutes to put on safety equipment if that means a little less productivity?
- Policies should be clearly communicated through the organization. It is not enough to just write policies. They must be disseminated and discussed throughout the organization.
- What is encouraged should be expected of everyone. Managers need to model the sorts of behavior expected. If assemblers are expected to wear safety gear on the shop floor, managers (and even visiting executives) should too.
- Climate needs to be discussed. This discussion should occur at all levels. To build an ethical climate, for example, ethics needs to be a frequent topic of conversation at staff meetings. Ethical lapses reported in the news, even from other companies, can be a good conversation starter.
- Supervisors should take corrective action. When employees engage in behaviors that are discouraged, supervisors should take appropriate corrective action. Depending on the seriousness of the breach, this might be just a friendly discussion of the situation and how the employee might have better handled it. Such incidents can also be the topic of conversation at a staff meeting, not to embarrass individuals, but to help employees understand what is expected.

Culture is often referred to as the unique "personality" of an organization. If that is true, then organizational climate is the mood of your organization. Whereas culture is the system of values and beliefs that determine how a company's employees and management interact, the climate is how your employees experience that culture (Chen 2019).

Glisson (2015) offers the "ARC" (availability, responsiveness, and continuity) model as a means to connect organizational climate and change. The first ARC strategy embeds five *principles* of effectiveness (e.g., results-oriented, mission-driven) within the organization to guide ongoing organizational innovation and service improvement efforts. The second ARC strategy promotes *shared mental models* (e.g., openness to change, psychological safety) among the staff to support service innovation and improvement efforts. The third ARC strategy trains teams in the use of *organizational component tools* (e.g., participatory decision making, the use of feedback) that are necessary to identify and address barriers to service innovation and effectiveness.

Glisson (2015) and others found five ARC principles to be particularly important in promoting successful innovation and effectiveness: (1) *be mission-driven, not rule-driven* where all actions and decisions contribute to improving the well-being of stakeholders; (2) *be results-oriented, not process-oriented*, where success is measured by how much results improves; (3) *be improvement-directed, not status quo-directed* by continually working to be more effective in improving the well-being of stakeholders; (4) *be relationship-centered, not individual-centered* by focusing on networks of relationships that affect service quality and collective results; and (5) *be participation-based, not authority-based* by involving key influential stakeholders early in designing change initiatives.

Change processes are represented by three ARC strategies (i.e., embedding guiding principles, developing shared mental models, and enacting organizational component tools) that are designed to improve organizational culture and climate and address organizational barriers while blending the intentions of practitioners with the organizational opportunities to achieve constructive change. This model supports the implementation of Evidence-based practices (EBPs) and other innovations by using change processes (ARC principles, mental models, and organizational tools) that affect organizational-level change mechanisms (organizational culture, climate, barriers) and individual-level change mechanisms (intentions) to influence individual behavior (e.g., innovation adoption) (Glisson 2015).

Climate may have a soft feel, but it has a measurable bottom-line impact. A positive climate improves individual engagement, enhancing performance and productivity while improving business results. A recent

Gallup poll about engagement found that 11 percent of employees were engaged, 62 percent were not engaged, and 27 percent were actively disengaged. Gallup's comparison of the climates of top versus bottom engagement quartiles demonstrated a clear link between engagement and productivity, profitability, and greater earnings per share (Walsh 2012).

Conversion

The final element, *conversion,* added during our test cases, refers to the ability of leaders to embed and sustain change, to convert the necessary adaptations into the natural DNA of the organization. Given the failure rates of change initiatives, as noted earlier, it is critical that leaders increase the probability that change initiatives will reach the expected outcomes, especially given the impact on precious resources. As Palmer, Dunford, and Akin (2009) note, for change to "stick" it must be "become the new normality." Nadler called this "baked in" and Kotter "the way we do things around here" (p. 355).

Organizations often spend an enormous amount of time and energy designing and building a future state, only to underinvest in the implementation and embedding of the changes into the "systems" of the organization. Leaders must ensure that focus and resource allocation are balanced and maintained across the end-to-end processes. A change management initiative only succeeds when the change in processes and outcomes becomes embedded in the day-to-day activities of the organization.

To be sustained, we must move from seeing change as a noun as noted earlier or as an event, it must be seen as normal and not "change" with the baggage that traditionally comes with the term (e.g., emotional, political, and negative connotations). There are a series of actions the effective change leader can take to embed or convert change into sustainable processes. These include: redesigning internal systems (e.g., reward, promotion, and recognition), redesigning roles, and linking decisions and behaviors to change objectives. Beer, Eisenstat, and Spector (1993) argue that the most behavior and attitudes are influenced by the context of roles, relationships, routines, and responsibilities (cited in Palmer, Dunford, and Akin, 2009, 360). Leaders should not expect change to be embedded by a conversion experience that focuses on attitude and beliefs, to be fully converted we must change the employee's day-to-day experiences.

As Morgan (2016) noted "When organizations ask me how long it takes to change or how long before they can really adapt to the future of work, my response is always 'right away and forever.'"

Quay Consulting (n.d.) listed these steps to engage staff and embed change in the organization's processes:

1. It starts from the top with strong and effective sponsorship from senior leaders.
2. Get the right people in the right places to ensure appropriate and fit-for-purpose resourcing.
3. Engage the business with "what's in it for me" through clear articulation and communication on the benefits for individuals, teams, and the organization.
4. Get engagement/buy-in from individuals, teams, and the organization by listening to and supporting the business concerns from all stakeholders across the business.
5. "Show, don't just tell": Excellent communication in all its forms (actions, behavior, spoken, written, group, and individual) need to demonstrate how change will benefit the business.
6. Be aligned: strong alignment between project managers and change managers is essential to ensure they are rowing the same boat.
7. Facilitate action and feedback by hearing concerns, taking action, and soliciting continual feedback.

We have to highlight again the critical role of the change vision to this conversion element. The change vision gives the organization a picture of what the future will look like after the change is embedded in the ways of working in the organization. It tells organizational stakeholders why they should let go of the past, sacrifice, and follow senior leadership into the future. If done correctly, the change vision creates an appealing picture of the future that provides guidance for organizational decision making and behaviors.

Kotter (2011) noted the differences between an organizational vision and the change vision.

If you are part of an organization that is trying to drive a large change, whether that's implementing a new IT system or moving to a new go-to-market strategy, you need to have a change vision. This is a picture for people of what the organization will look like after they have made significant changes, and it also shows them the opportunities they can take advantage of once they do that.

A change vision is not the same thing as a corporate vision. Both are important, but anyone who wants to successfully make a large-scale change in their organization needs to understand how they're different.

Every successful large-scale change that I have seen has, as a part of it, a change vision. And what that means is a picture of after we have made the changes on whatever dimensions, this is what we're going to look like. And if we look like that we're going to be able to exploit, grab, take advantage of some big opportunities over here that are a function of changes that are happening in this increasingly fast-moving world.

A generic corporate vision is where you think you need to look like out there on some fundamental dimensions to make you prosper. It's not about one specific large-scale change, it's about the future. And often, not always, that picture is about timeless values or principles, timeless behavior that makes organizations succeed. Increasingly, for example, one dimension of that timeless behavior is the embracing of change itself.

Another critical leadership action is the consistent and persistent alignment with the change vision by the leaders themselves. They must live the vision every day consistently and communicate the change vision consistently as well. Change words and change actions must match. If any inconsistency seeps in, confusion will also seep in and this will lead to indecision, inaction, inertia, and potentially a loss of credibility, all of which will undermine the change vision. Leaders have to demonstrate an unwavering commitment to the change vision but with a dose of flexibility as mentioned earlier on the importance of adaptability (Kelley 2016).

It is important to conversion that the change initiative be seen as working. There is always some doubt initially, especially given the high failure rates. Using appropriate metrics to track progress can serve several important functions. It can create positive momentum, it can offer "proof" to the naysayers or doubters that the initiative may indeed work, it can serve as an early warning system that something is off track and allow for proactive intervention, and finally, it can fuel interim opportunities for recognition and celebration, which will add to the momentum.

It is also critical to conversion that employees up and down the organization "own" the change. This means they must "buy-in" to the change vision and also feel some responsibility for the expected outcomes. This can be accomplished in several ways including early and meaningful participation in the development of the change vision. A meaningful level of responsibility and accountability for the change initiative's success is also critical, giving the employees a "voice" in the actual implementation plan.

The C^6 framework is not intended to dictate a specific approach to change leadership. It is meant to use lessons from the adaptive enterprise to promote the creation of an organizational environment that will foster adaptability as a means to reduce the negative impact of serial or ill-defined changes. The "C^6" change management framework has been offered as a means for leaders to create firm-specific change leadership approaches enabled with practices related to the 6 "Cs." The specific purpose of the framework is to infuse adaptability into the organizational DNA. Leaders will need to adapt and tailor this framework to the situation they face and the organization's culture, assets, and competencies.

The prior version of the C^6 framework (C^5) has been deployed in two cases. The two cases, although limited in duration, demonstrated the framework has value in practice. The feedback from the participants in the process was very positive, and the tangible measures used to evaluate the change initiatives were all above expectations. For example, in one of the cases at eight months, the CEO noted, "A much smoother acquisition than expected; no negative financial impact, employee surveys are up and customer 'promoter' scores are better than expected." The representative from the parent company said, "By previous acquisition experiences—this acquisition has had a more significant positive impact."

The model was developed and deployed in two cases in 2008 and again in 2015: in a small software firm (70 people) facing a turnaround led by a new CEO as well as a medium-sized firm (1,100 employees) following an acquisition. The results suggest the model may have applicability as a means to lead change and to mitigate the related stressors. Because of confidentiality constraints, we can only offer an overview of the case results, without citations.

In the first case, a new CEO was brought in after two failed turnaround initiatives by the primary investor. He decided to deploy the C^5 model to launch a new series of change initiatives with the goals of meeting financial expectations and to improve employee engagement. He devoted considerable personal time over a five-month period in leading the model. He deployed tactics and initiatives in each of the "C" elements.

> For *Communication* he convened a meeting of key influencers and held a pre-announcement workshop. He then had a kickoff meeting with the entire staff, followed up with weekly updates (email) and every other Friday live updates. The CFO issued financial updates each week ("Friday Scorecards") and whiteboards were documented with updates. Finally, the CEO spent a lot of time amongst employees creating dialogue on the changes.
>
> In terms of *Confidence*, the CEO and his leadership team continually stressed that the changes would work and used what Kotter (1996) calls "small wins" to build momentum. They highlighted progress using specific examples and the use of milestones. For *Cohesion*, they ran a series of team building events as well as appointed employee leaders for specific projects ensuring the "voice of the employee," as the CEO called it, was a prominent element in the change process.
>
> In terms of *Collaboration*, employee-led work teams were established for process analysis and improvements and an Employee Council was set up to meet with the CEO monthly, as examples. Finally, in terms of *Climate*, as stated earlier, small wins were publicly shared and celebrated, expectations were realistic but confidently expressed, rewards were given for specific contributions and missteps were shared without the assignment of blame.
>
> At 6 months, the financial targets had been met, the organizational environment changed for the better and employee retention was better than the prior experience. From the CEO, "The results

were better than expected in terms of cohesion, cooperation and attitude. Not sure it helped as much as it could in tangible results in such a short period but the effect overall was certainly positive."

Employee comments included:

"It felt like we were it in together all the way. He (CEO) made us part of it."

"We did a lot in a short period. I wasn't sure we could do it but we did."

"I had information I did not have with the other CEO, it was worse than I thought, but at least I knew."

In the other case, an 1,100-person firm recently acquired by a Fortune 20 company. The acquiring company decided to use the model to ensure a "smooth transition." The model was deployed for an eight-month period in late 2014 and early 2015. In this case, the CEO of the acquired company led the C^5 process along with members of the senior executive team and an executive from the acquirer. In this case, the process started with an extensive review of the performance to date of the company using an array of financial, operational, and human capital (e.g., retention rates) metrics. They also used industry benchmarks to calibrate the metrics as well as employee surveys and customer "promoter" score (an internally developed customer survey process). From this, they developed an "expectations scorecard" and a definition of "success" (both of which have been kept confidential).

For the *Communications* element, they deployed similar activities as the smaller company (e.g., weekly "integration" updates, white board announcements) but added in a few unique items as well (extensive use of an Intranet site, "Ask the CEO" anonymous site, monthly Town Hall meetings and a CEO monthly podcast). Other leaders also held similar communication events at the functional levels. For the *Confidence* element, they also used milestone progress as a means to celebrate "small wins," as well as extensive publication of the "expectations scorecard" with weekly updates using a "stop light" format (green for on-target, yellow for slightly off target and red for areas needing attention).

In terms of *Collaboration*, they formed a "Steering Commit-tee" of selected managers and key employees from up, down and across the organization as well as three representatives from the new parent company. They formed an "Integration" team as well as 13 sub-teams of managers and employees to work on vari-ous integration elements (e.g., a team on "systems," another on "employee transition"). They also set up three "Employee Coun-cils," on each on their three main sites. These employee councils met with the CEO or a senior executive monthly.

For *Cohesion,* they used the various integration teams, some smaller sub-cross functional teams and a mentoring ("buddy") process to link up managers and employees from the acquired company and the acquirer. Finally, in terms of *Climate*, they used recognition, an extensive feedback process (tracking of sugges-tions), an unambiguous presentation of expectations and a series of "celebration" events around milestone accomplishment.

At eight months, the CEO noted, "A much smoother acqui-sition than expected; no negative financial impact, employee surveys are up and customer "promoter" scores are better than expected." The representative from the parent company said, "By previous acquisition experiences—this acquisition has had a more significant positive impact."

Employee comments included:

"We have a lot of adapting to do but so far it has been fine and if I am honest, better than I expected."

"They are a much bigger company and as a result things take longer but they seem to be willing to adapt to our practices when they are better."

"They have the assets we needed and are willing to invest in us which is what we needed. They treat us as adults and we have influenced the priorities. I appreciate the "no-BS" approach to information—we are not excluded."

Tangibly, at eight months, the acquisition was ahead of the expecta-tions scorecard on eight of the nine measures, retention was better than expected (only one of the 13 member management team of the acquired company had left) and "stress indicators" (from employee surveys) were within preacquisition range.

Given the persistent conditions noted in our earlier "Speed of Now" section, there is no indication that change is going to slow down anytime soon, or that systemic impatience will dissipate. Therefore, we believe our *C⁶ Change Leadership Framework* can be successfully deployed by leaders to embed adaptability into the natural DNA of the organization.

CHAPTER 10

Bringing It All Together

Shifting Change From a Noun to a Verb

The presence of the environmental stressors mentioned earlier suggests that most organizations will have to adjust (change) to meet these conditions in such a manner that will either be continuous or so frequent as to seem continuous (Arena 2002; Senge, Kleiner, Roberts, Ross, Roth, and Smith 1999; Ashkenas, Ulrich, Jick, and Kerr 2002). The demands of the organization's stakeholders and market forces create pressure on management to act. Waterson, Clegg, Bolden, Pepper, Warr and Wallet (1999) noted that organizations have been taking on a wide range of change initiatives to compete in this environment and the trend does not appear to be abating.

Kelley (2016) noted this as well: "When an organizations capacity for change absorption is exceeded by its pace of change, then the organization has reached the point of change saturation."

As noted earlier, many firms are launching persistent (serial or overlapping) change initiatives in response to stressors in the environment. Clearly, one way to reduce the negative effects of *continuous change* and change saturation is to reduce the number of change initiatives launched by the organization. If recent history is a guide, this seems unlikely. The systemic impatience between organizational leaders and their stakeholders as well as the volatility in the environment indicates that depending on a reduction in change initiatives is not a reasonable position. It would certainly help and should be encouraged but another approach needs to be pursued.

An alternative to reducing the number of change initiatives is to reframe the notion of "change" and to create a change leadership framework that encourages a more adaptive and flexible organization.

One of the challenges to the interpretation of the theoretical change models is that it is often assumed a "one-size-fits-all" approach. This is unrealistic. Change may have many common characteristics, but, in practice,

change is a situational and a specific experience for employees and the organization. Change management programs seem to be most effective when
they are organization-specific. Therefore, the new offering suggested here
is a "framework," not a specific model. It is meant as a means to "frame"
organizational strategies, processes, and tactics, in order to improve the
organization's flexibility, agility, and to reduce the stress related to change.
The framework combines elements of the adaptive enterprise with additional input from change theorists such as Kotter (1996) who emphasizes
the concepts of visioning, communication, and anchoring.

Sinek (2019) offers the notion of "existential flexibility" as an organizational value. He defines it as the capacity to initiate disruption to
a business model or a strategic cause. He makes the point that this is
essential to advance a "just cause" (change vision). The leader with an
"infinite mindset" has an appreciation for the unpredictable and will flex
as needed.

Kelley (2016) argues that change should be seen as an "investment."
If adaptability is embedded into the organizational DNA and seen as a
natural part of the daily processes of the organization, it is likely that the
organization will develop the resilience to successfully navigate the challenges of the "speed of now."

Kelley (2016) goes on to say that as the "pace of change accelerates
and the nature of change continues to evolve the more forward-thinking
and adaptable organizations will take a different approach to change." He
offers "Eight Principles of Continued Change Success":

1. Change needs to be "expected" and part of the natural process of the
   organization.
2. Change needs to become "part of the fabric" of the organization.
3. Change strategies, programs, or initiatives need to be characterized
   by "transparency."
4. Change needs to be a "collaborative" process.
5. Change needs to be a commitment but with a dose of flexibility.
6. Change must be agile to meet the "speed of now."
7. Change must be drive by stakeholder need.
8. Change must be "built to scale" and be contextually and situation-
   ally appropriate.

Ayelet Baron (Kelley 2016) is a futurist who often writes on the notion of "change is abundant" in the 21st century. She notes that some still see change as program that can be "neatly tied in a bow," but in reality, change must become a "way of life" for an organization to remain relevant.

To emphasize her points Table 10.1 offers a contrast between the mindsets of a 20th Century organization and the needed mindsets for the 21st Century.

Table 10.1 The shift in organization's adaptability approach

20th Century Organizations	21st Century Organizations
Deficit mindset: There is not enough Competing	Abundance mindset; We have enough Collaborating
Sponsorship: ask leaders to sponsor the change	Conscious leaders own and integrate change into the business
Managed and delegated the change program	Integrated into the business with strategic partners
On-way communication to audiences	Storytelling and conversations with communities
Resistance to change	Work and adapt to changing business needs
Measure activity	Measure impact

In addition to highlighting the modalities, realities, and adaptability of change within an organization, this book also aims to highlight the fact that leadership of change is critical to success. An agile workforce is based on the agility of the leaders of the organization at large. In the past, particularly the 20th century, leaders could set a tone and expect that employees in an organization would march to the beat of their drum. While that may have been the case in a lot of situations, today, a leader is expected to be not only the person setting the direction but also to be participatory in the change, provide transparency of the what, why, and how of changes, and actively be seen to live out the tenets of the change on both a professional and personal level, all the while keeping a close eye on public opinion of themselves and the organization. Hiring an experienced CEO is no longer enough; hiring an experienced CEO who is adept at communicating and participatory in the life of the organization at large has become a nonnegotiable trait required of leaders today.

Emotional intelligence, strength of character, and personal characteristics such as patients, empathy, resilience, and grit have transcended buzzword status and have become essential to leaderships for companies both small and large. To be fair, the change leader cannot do all of this themselves. As such, much of these characteristics need to be leveraged to empower and transfer change objectives to a full leadership team. When leaders and their media teams are able to be on the same page and walk lockstep with each other on any change plans, it provides the organization with the highest likelihood of success and the resilience needed to face continuous change. In today's world, one can consider this the "event horizon" management skills, or perhaps one of the more sought-after skills of leaders in today's economy. Can the leader not only embody all these facets of effective change management, but can they also transfer this philosophy, work ethic, and sense of transparency to their leadership team? Leaders capable of both embodying all the skills and traits discussed in this book while also having the aptitude of coalescing the leadership team around them will likely be the most sought-after combination of experiences for CEO positions today and into the near future.

Finally, there is the need to mold an organization into an adaptive organization. As we discussed in earlier chapters, changing the culture of the company when it has been used to operating in the status quo is one of the most difficult things to do. Embedding into the culture the value of experimentation, risk-taking, and flexibility in decision making all take time and can sometimes be a never-ending pursuit. After all, companies are made up of people and people are unpredictable when adopting the change. In previous decades, issuing a memo to the entire organization highlighting change initiatives may have been sufficient. Today, employees are far more independent in thought and opinion. In flexibility can set in quickly and be very difficult to change. And while distributed leadership in the ability for mid-level managers to make independent decisions may sound very useful, trust becomes a major factor in whether these managers and teams can truly believe that they can make decisions and take risks without repudiation. All of this is to say, developing a change mindset is both beneficial and elusive. The resilience needed to make change a constant feature involves emotions, personal adjustments, and putting the status quo in the rearview.

References

Abrahamson, E. 2004. "Avoiding Repetitive Change Syndrome." *MIT Sloan Development Review* 45, no. 2, pp. 93–95. www.imaworldwide.com/blog/5-shocking-truths-about-resistance-to-change (accessed May 21, 2021).

Aims, J., T. Slack, and C. Hinings. 2017. "The Pace, Sequence and Linearity of Radical Change." *Academy of Management Journal* 47, no. 1.

Akins, N. 2020. "Keys to Building Change Resilience for You and Your Team." https://trainingindustry.com/magazine/jan-feb-2020/5-keys-to-building-change-resilience-for-you-and-your-team/ (accessed May 20, 2021).

Alsher, P. 2015. "5 Shocking Truths about Resistance to Change."

American Management Association. January 24, 2019. "Creating Adaptive Organizations." *AMA*. www.amanet.org/articles/creating-adaptive-organizations/

Arena, M. 2002. "Changing the Way We Change." *Organization Development Journal* 20, no. 2, pp. 33–48.

Armenakis, A., and A. Bedelan. 1999. "Organizational Change: A Review of Theory and Research in the 1990s." *Journal of Management* 25, no. 3, pp. 293–315.

Ashkenas, R., D. Ulrich, T. Jick, and S. Kerr. 2002. "The Boundaryless Organization." San Francisco: Jossey-Bass.

Bareil, C., A. Savoie, and S. Meunier. 2007. "Patterns of Discomfort with Organizational Change." *Journal of Change Management* 7, no. 1, pp. 13–34.

Beer, M., and N. Nohria. 2000. *Purpose of Change*. Boston: Harvard Business School Press.

Beer, M., R. Eisenstat, and B. Spector. 1993. *Managing Change*. New York, NY: Sage.

Bennett, N. and G. Lemoine. 2014. "What VUCA Means for You." https://hbr.org/2014/01/what-vuca-really-means-for-you (accessed February 07, 2021).

Blanchard. n.d. "Leadership Strategies or Making Change Stick." Available from www.blanchard.com.tr/Uploads/files/Arastirma/leadership-strategies-for-making-change-stick.pdf (accessed March 11, 2022).

Blodget, H. 2015. "CEO Jeff Immelt on Transforming GE." www.yahoo.com/lifestyle/ceo-jeff-immelt-transforming-ge-162739186.html (accessed May 21, 2021).

Brower, T. 2020. "Want to Manage Change Successfully." *Separate These 5 Myths from Realities*. www.forbes.com/sites/tracybrower/2020/02/14/want-to-manage-change-successfully-separate-these-5-myths-from-realities/?sh=834eea675d32 (accessed May 21, 2021).

B-Team. 2015. "New Ways of Working." https://bteam.org/ (accessed May 21, 2021).

Buchanan, D. 2003. "Demands, Instabilities, Manipulations, Careers: The Lived Experience of Driving Change." *Human Relations* 56, no. 6, pp. 663–684.

Bureau of Labor Statistics. 2018. "Women in the Workforce." www.bls.gov/opub/ted/women.htm (accessed May 18, 2021).

Cap Gemini/Ernst, and Young. 2005. "The Case for IT Agility and Ecosystem Integration." Available at August 28, 2005, from www.capgemini.com/adaptive

Cap Gemini/Ernst, and Young. May 2003. "CEO Viewpoints: The Adaptive Enterprise." , and Young. 2005. "The Case for IT Agility and Ecosystem Integration." Available August 25, 2005, from www.capgemini.com/adaptive

Capece, D. November 21, 2019. "Why Adaptability is the Key Ingredient to Leadership Success." *Wharton Magaz*ine. https://magazine.wharton.upenn.edu/digital/why-adaptability-is-the-key-ingredient-to-leadership-success/

Carr, A., and P. Hancock. 2006. "Space and Time in Organizational Change Management." *Journal of Organizational Change Management* 34, no. 3.

Center for Creative Leadership. n.d. "How to Be a Successful Change Leader." and Young. 2005. "The Case for IT Agility and Ecosystem Integration." Available at March 17, 2020 from www.ccl.org/articles/leading-effectively-articles/successful-change-leader/

Chen, D. 2019. "Organizational Climate." https://talkingtalent.prosky.co/articles/organizational-climate (accessed April 04, 2021).

Cisco. 2011. "Transitioning to Workforce 2020." www.cisco.com/c/dam/en_us/about/ac49/ac55/docs/Workforce_2020_White_Paper_012411.pdf (accessed May 21, 2021).

Clear, J. n.d. "The Science of Developing Mental Toughness in Your Health, Work and Life." Available from https://jamesclear.com/mental-toughness (accessed March 12, 2022).

Clegg, S. R., M. Kornberger, and T. Pitsis. 2011. *Managing and Organizations: An Introduction to Theory and Practice*. Thousand Oaks, CA: Sage Publications.

Corporate Finance Institute. (2018, November 12). "Adaptive Leadership." https://corporatefinanceinstitute.com/resources/careers/soft-skills/adaptive-leadership/

Costanza, D.P., N. Blacksmith, M.R. Coats, J.B. Severt, and A.H. DeCostanza. 2016. "The Effect of Adaptive Organizational Culture on Long-Term Survival." *Journal of Business and Psychology* 31, no. 3, pp. 361–381. https://doi.org/10.1007/s10869-015-9420-y

Coutu, D. 2002. *How Resilience Works*. Harvard Business Review.

Creately. 2021. "The Easy Guide to the McKinsey 7S Model." https://creately.com/blog/diagrams/mckinsey-7s-model-guide/ (accessed March 31, 2021).

Cross, R. 2021. *Beyond Collaboration Overload.* Boston: Harvard Business Review Press.

Cserti, R. 2019. "Essential Facilitation Skills for an Effective Facilitator." and Young. 2005. "The Case for IT Agility and Ecosystem Integration." Available at March 30, 2020, from www.sessionlab.com/blog/facilitation-skills/

Daniels, G., and C. Hollfield. 2002. "Times of Turmoil: Short and Long-Term Effects of Organizational Change on Newsroom Employees." *Journalism & Mass Communication Quarterly* 79, no. 3, pp. 661–680.

Davis, S. 2000. "Blur: The Speed of Change in the Connected Economy." www.researchgate.net/publication/234805880_Blur_The_Speed_of_Change_in_the_Connected_Economy (accessed May 18, 2021).

Denning, S. 2018. *The Age of Agile.* New York, NY: AMACON.

Dent, E., and S. Goldberg. 1999."Challenging Resistance to Change." *The Journal of Applied Behavioral Science* 35, no. 1, pp. 25–42.

Devries, H. 2017. "Mistakes to Avoid When Communicating Change." Available at March 14. 2021, from https://icma.org/articles/pm-magazine/mistakes-avoid-when-communicating-change-0?gclid=EAIaIQobChMIsYGeldaw7wIVEDizAB092QVxEAMYASAAEgJfA_D_BwE

Do, B., P. Yeh, and J. Madsen. 2016. "Exploring the Relationship Among Human Resource Flexibility, Organizational Innovation and Adaptability Culture." *Chinese Management Studies* 10, no. 4, pp. 657–674. https://doi.org/10.1108/cms-01-2016-0022

Dool, R. 2006. *Enervative Change.* Berlin: VDM: Verlag Dr. Muller.

Dool, R. 2021. *Leaderocity™: Leading at the Speed of Now.* New York, NY: Business Expert Press.

Duckworth, A. 2016. *Grit: The Power of Passion and Perseverance.* New York, NY: Scribner.

Dweck, C. January 2016. *What Having a 'Growth Mindset' Actually Means.* Harvard Business Review.

Dwoskin, E. May 23, 2016. *Behind Yahoo's Downfall: Bad Bets and Failure to Adapt.* Chicagotribune.Com. www.chicagotribune.com/business/blue-sky/ct-behind-yahoos-downfall-20160420-story.html

Dym, B., and H. Hutson. n.d.. "Leveraging Organizational Readiness for Change." https://thesystemsthinker.com/leveraging-organizational-readiness-for-change/ (accessed April 02, 2021).

Erwin, D., and A. Garman. 2010. "Resistance to Organizational Change: Linking Research and Practice." *Leadership and Organizational Development Journal* 21, no. 1, pp. 39–56.

Expert Program Management (EPM). n.d.. "ADKAR Model of Change." https://expertprogrammanagement.com/2018/02/adkar-model-of-change/ (accessed March 31, 2021).

Forbes. 2014. "Half Of Companies Not Ready For Transformational Change, Says New Study By Forbes Insights And Medidata." www.forbes.com/sites/forbespr/2014/06/23/half-of-companies-not-ready-for-transformational-change-says-new-study-by-forbes-insights-and-medidata/?sh=2a3dca4513b2

Fortuna, C. March 22, 2021. "The Digital Age & EVs—Rethinking & Revitalizing Transportation." *CleanTechnica.* https://cleantechnica.com/2021/03/22/the-digital-age-evs-rethinking-revitalizing-transportation/

Friedman, T. 2016. "Thank You for Being Late: An Optimist's Guide to Thriving in the Age of Accelerations." New York, NY: Farrar, Straus and Giroux.

Garelli, S. 2016. "Why You Will Probably Live Longer than Most Big Companies." www.imd.org/research-knowledge/articles/why-you-will-probably-live-longer-than-most-big-companies/ (accessed November 23, 2021).

Garvin, D. July–August 1993. "Building a Learning Organization." *Harvard Business Review*, pp. 78–91.

Gibson, K., K. O'Leary, and J. Weintraub. 2020. "The Little Things That Make Employees Feel Appreciated." Available at March 16, 2020, from https://hbr.org/2020/01/the-little-things-that-make-employees-feel-appreciated?utm_medium=social&utm_campaign=hbr&utm_source=linkedin

Gill, J., and S. Whittle. 1992. "Management by Panacea: Accounting for Transcience." *Journal of Management Studies* 30, no. 2.

Glisson, C. 2015. "The Role of Organizational Culture and Climate in Innovation and Effectiveness." *Human Services Organizational Leadership* 39, no. 4, pp. 245–250.

Goman, C.K. July 11, 2017. "Six Crucial Behaviors of Collaborative Leaders." Available at April 25, 2020, from www.forbes.com/sites/carolkinseygoman/2017/07/11/six-crucial-behaviors-of-collaborative-leaders/#6e1c30fb8cbe

Greenwood, R., and C. Hinings. 1996. "Understanding Radical Organizational Change: Bringing Together the Old and New Institutionalism." *Academy of Management* 21, no. 4.

Gronn, P. 2002. "Distributed Leadership." *Second International Handbook of Educational Leadership and Administration,* pp. 653–696. https://doi.org/10.1007/978-94-010-0375-9_23

Guastello, S.J. 2013. *Chaos, Catastrophe, and Human Affairs: Applications of Nonlinear Dynamics to Work, Organizations, and Social Evolution.* New York, NY: Psychology Press.

Guzman, N., M. Prema, R. Sood, and D. Wilkes. December 17, 2020. "Coronavirus' Impact on Service Organizations: Weathering the Storm." McKinsey & Company. www.mckinsey.com/business-functions/operations/our-insights/coronavirus-impact-on-service-organizations-weathering-the-storm#

Gwynne, P. 1997. "Skunk Works, 1990s-Style." *Research-Technology Management* 40, no. 4, pp. 18–23. https://doi.org/10.1080/08956308.1997.11671138

Hamel, G., and N. Tennant. April 27, 2015. "The 5 Requirements of a Truly Innovative Company." *Harvard Business Review.* https://hbr.org/2015/04/the-5-requirements-of-a-truly-innovative-company

Hammer, M., and J. Champy. 2009. *Reengineering the Corporation: A Manifesto for Business Revolution.* New York, NY: HarperBusiness Essentials.

Healthfield, S. 2021a. "What is Resistance to Change." www.thebalancecareers.com/communication-in-change-management-1917805 (accessed May 14, 2021).

Heathfield, S. 2021b. "Communication in Change Management." Available at March 14, 2021 from www.thebalancecareers.com/communication-in-change-management-1917805

Heerwagen, J., K. Kelly, and K. Kampschroer. 2006. "The Changing Nature of Organizations, Work and Workplace." *Whole Building Design Guide.* www.wbdg.org/resources/chngorgwork.php (accessed June 20, 2021).

Heflo. n.d.. "Organizational Climate Definition: Everything You Need to Know." www.heflo.com/blog/hr/organizational-climate-definition/ (accessed June 20, 2021).

Heifetz, R.A., M. Linsky, and A. Grashow. 2009. *The Practice of Adaptive Leadership: Tools and Tactics for Changing Your Organization and the World,* 1st ed. Harvard Business Press.

Higgs, M., and D. Rowland. 2000. "Building Change Leadership Capability: The Quest for Change Competence." *Journal of Change Management* 1, no. 2, pp. 116–130.

Hoag, B., H. Ritschard, and G. Coper. 2002. "Obstacles to Effective Organizational Change: The Underlying Reasons." *Leadership and Organizational Development Journal* 42, no. 5.

Holland, J. August 19, 2016. "4 Characteristics of Adaptive Sales Organizations." *Entrepreneur.* www.entrepreneur.com/article/279935

Hope, J., P. Bunce, and F. Röösli. 2011. *The Leader's Dilemma.* Wiley.

Hughes, M. 2011. "Do 70 Per Cent of all Organizational Change Initiatives Really Fail?" *Journal of Change Management* 11, no. 4, pp. 451–464.

Hugos, M.H. 2009. *Business Agility: Sustainable Prosperity in a Relentlessly Competitive World.* Hoboken, NJ: John Wiley & Sons.

Hutzschenreuter, T., and I. Kleindienst. 2006. *Journal of Management* 32, no. 5, pp. 673–720.

Indeed. 2021. "10 Steps To Improve Team Cohesiveness in the Workplace." www.indeed.com/career-advice/career-development/team-cohesiveness (accessed April 02, 2021).

Indeed. February 22, 2021. "What Is Adaptive Leadership?" *Indeed Career Guide.* www.indeed.com/career-advice/career-development/adaptive-leadership

Insights. n.d. "Remaining Resilient through Change." www.insights.com/us/resources/remaining-resilient-through-change/ (accessed May 15, 2021).

Institute for the Future. 2011. "Future Work Skills 2020." www.iftf.org/futureworkskills/ (accessed June 15, 2021).

Jason, J. 2020. "The 7S Framework—An Application to Coca Cola." [Online] Available at https://businessleadershipmanagement.wordpress.com/2013/06/11/the-7s-framework/

Jick, T. 1991b. *Implementing Change. Note 9-494-083.* Boston: Harvard Business School Press.

Jimmieson, N., D. Terry, and V. Callan. 2004. "A Longitudinal Study of Employee Adaptation to Organizational Change: The Role of Change-Related Information and Change-Related Self-Efficacy." *Journal of Occupational Health Psychology* 9, no. 1, pp. 11–27.

Johnson, W. 2020. *4 Benefits of Sharing Information in the Workplace.* Available at March 18, 2020, from https://smallbiztrends.com/2017/01/benefits-of-sharing-information-in-the-workplace.html

Keating, K. March 10, 2021. "3 Traits of Adaptable Leaders." Association of Talent Development. www.td.org/insights/3-traits-of-adaptable-leaders

Keller, S., and B. Schaninger. 2019. *Beyond Performance 2.0.* New York, NY: John Wiley & Sons.

Kelley, B. 2016. *Charting Change: A Visual Toolkit for Making Change Stick.* London: Palgrave Macmillan.

Kishore, S.H.T. August 07, 2015. "The Power of Incremental Innovation." *WIRED.* www.wired.com/insights/2013/11/the-power-of-incremental-innovation/

Kotler, P., and J. Casilone. 2009. *Chaotics: The Business of Managing and Marketing in the Age of Turbulence.* New York, NY: Amacom.

Kotter, J. 1996. *Leading change.* Cambridge: Harvard Business School Press.

Kotter, J. 2011. *How to Create a Powerful Vision for Change.* www.forbes.com/sites/johnkotter/2011/06/07/how-to-create-a-powerful-vision-for-change/?sh=1833de4151fc (accessed April 06, 2021).

Kotter, J. 2014. *Accelerate: Building Strategic Agility for a Faster Moving World.* Boston, MA: Harvard Business Review Press.

Krane, J., and K.B. Medlock. 2018. "Geopolitical Dimensions of US Oil Security." *Energy Policy* 114, pp. 558–565. https://doi.org/10.1016/j.enpol.2017.12.050

LaReau, J.L. March 12, 2021. "GM Forms New Joint Venture to Fast-Track EV Battery Development." *Detroit Free Press.* https://eu.freep.com/story/money/cars/general-motors/2021/03/11/gm-electric-vehicle-battery-development/4647250001/

Lau, C., D. Tse, and N. Zhou. 2002. "Institutional Forces and Organizational Culture in China: Effects on Change Schemas, Firm Commitment and Job Satisfaction." *Journal of International Business Studies* 33, no. 3, pp. 533–551.

Leana, C., and B. Barry. 2000. "Stability and Change as Simultaneous Experiences in Organizational Life [Editorial]." *The Academy of Management Review* 25, no. 4, pp. 753–759.

Lewin, K. 1947. "Frontiers in Group Dynamics: I. Concept, Method and Reality in Social Sciences; Social Equilibria and Social Change." *Human Relations* 1, pp. 5–41.

Li, J.-Y., R. Sun, W. Tao, and Y. Lee. 2021. "Employee Coping with Organizational Change in the Face of a Pandemic: The Role of Transparent Internal Communication." *Public Relations Review* 47, no. 1, p. 101984. https://doi.org/10.1016/j.pubrev.2020.101984

Little, J. 2015. "3 Reasons Why You Should Build Your Own Change Method." https://leanchange.org/2015/05/3-reasons-why-you-should-build-your-own-change-method/ (accessed March 31, 2021).

Lombardi, D. 1997. *Reorganization and Renewal: Strategies for Healthcare Leaders.* Chicago: American College of Healthcare Executives.

Loten, A. October 24, 2020. "Home Depot Won a Lot of Customers During the Pandemic. The Trick Is Keeping Them." *WSJ.* www.wsj.com/articles/home-depot-won-a-lot-of-customers-during-the-pandemic-the-trick-is-keeping-them-11603533601

Macaulay, S. n.d. "No One is an Island: How Successful Leaders Effect Change through Collaboration." https://blog.som.cranfield.ac.uk/execdev/effect-change-through-collaboration (accessed April 01, 2021).

Mahoney, M. March 18, 2021. "The Impact of Social Media on Business in 2021." *Single Grain.* www.singlegrain.com/blog-posts/impact-of-social-media-in-todays-business-world/

Mai, R., and A. Akerson. 2003. *The Leader As Communicator.* New York, NY: AMACOM.

Mallon, D. February 28, 2020. "Getting Decision Rights Right." *Deloitte Insights.* www2.deloitte.com/us/en/insights/topics/talent/organizational-decision-making.html

Markowitz, B.A. March 12, 2021. "13 Iconic Retailers That Have Fallen Into Bankruptcy." *AARP.* www.aarp.org/money/credit-loans-debt/info-2020/bankrupt-retail-chain-store-list-is-growing.html

Maurer, I. 2010. "How to Build Trust in Inter-Organizational Projects." *International Journal of Project Management* 28, no. 7, pp. 629–637.

MBO Partners. 2011. "Independent Workforce Trends." www.mbopartners.com/blog/category/independent-workforce-trends/ (accessed May 22, 2021).

McKinsey & Company. 2015. "How to Beat the Transformation Odds. www.mckinsey.com/business-functions/organization/our-insights/how-to-beat-the-transformation-odds (accessed May 15, 2021).

McKinsey & Company. 2019. "Getting Personal About Change." www.mckinsey.com/business-functions/organization/our-insights/getting-personal-about-change (accessed May 15, 2021).

McKinsey & Company. 2020. "Ready, Set, Go: Reinventing the Organization for Speed in the Post-COVID-19 Era." www.mckinsey.com/business-functions/organization/our-insights/ready-set-go-reinventing-the-organization-for-speed-in-the-post-covid-19-era# (accessed April 13, 2021).

Meister, J., and Willyerd. 2010. *The 2020 Workplace*: New York, NY: HarperCollins e-books.

Miller, D. 2002. "Successful Change Leaders: What Makes Them? What Do They Do that is Different." *Journal of Change Management* 2, no. 4, pp. 359–369.

Minaar, J. November 22, 2020. "5 Best Practices To Distribute Decision-Making." *Corporate Rebels*. https://corporate-rebels.com/distribute-decision-making/

Morgan, J. 2016. *How Long Does Organizational Change Actually Take?* www.forbes.com/sites/jacobmorgan/2016/02/12/how-long-does-organizational-change-actually-take/?sh=6fdb23b17952 (accessed April 06, 2021).

Murphy, B. January 05, 2019. "People Think Netflix Killed Blockbuster. Now a New Report Says These 7 Other Things Mattered More." *Inc.Com*. www.inc.com/bill-murphy-jr/people-think-netflix-killed-blockbuster-now-a-brand-new-report-says-these-7-other-things-mattered-more.html

Murphy, M. 2016. "New Data Shows That Leaders Overestimate How Much Their Employees Want To Change." www.forbes.com/sites/markmurphy/2016/02/19/new-data-shows-that-leaders-overestimate-how-much-their-employees-want-to-change/?sh=67a5c24f162f (accessed May 21, 2021).

Nazar, J. April 21, 2021. "13 Leadership Lessons from Zoom Founder and CEO Eric Yuan." Entrepreneur. www.entrepreneur.com/article/368550

NCBI. n.d. "Aging and the Macroeconomy." www.ncbi.nlm.nih.gov/books/NBK148824/ (accessed May 21, 2021).

Nelson, A., and C. Cooper. 1995. "Uncertainty Amidst Change: The Impact of Privatization on Employee Job Satisfaction and Well-Being." *Journal of Occupational & Organizational Psychology* 68, no. 1, pp. 57–72.

Nelson, K. 2011. "Change Management: Understanding the Human Dynamics of Change." www.pmi.org/learning/library/change-management-understanding-human-dynamics-6252 (accessed May 28, 2021).

Newman, K. 2000. "Organizational Transformational During Institutional Upheaval." *Academy of Management* 25, no. 3.

Newton, R. 2017. "Five Ways to Drive Collaborative Change in Your Organization." https://blogs.lse.ac.uk/management/2017/07/31/five-ways-to-drive-collaborative-change-in-your-organisation/ (accessed April 01, 2021).

Nivel, A. December 18, 2020. "These Were the Companies that Best Adapted to the Crisis of this Year 2020." Entrepreneur. www.entrepreneur.com/article/361975

Nixon, S. August 28, 2020. "Global Integration Is More Important than Ever to Contain the Economic and Health Fallout and Exit the COVID-19 Pandemic Crisis." *World Bank Group*. https://openknowledge.worldbank.org/handle/10986/34394

Nobl. n.d.. "Successful Change Requires an Understanding of Organizational Psychology." https://nobl.io/organizational-change-management?gclid=EAIaIQobChMIxa7yl6fd8AIVIevjBx2ceQOCEAMYASAAEgKR8_D_BwE (accessed May 21, 2021).

Ovans, A. 2015. "What Resilience Means and Why It Matters." https://hbr.org/2015/01/what-resilience-means-and-why-it-matters (accessed April 02, 2021).

Palmer, I., R. Dunford, and G. Akin. 2009. *Managing Organizational Change*. New York, NY: McGraw-Hill/Irwin.

Patel, N. 2015. "90% of Startups Fail: Here's What You Need to Know About the 10%." Available from www.forbes.com/sites/neilpatel/2015/01/16/90-of-startups-will-fail-heres-what-you-need-to-know-about-the-10/?sh=5ad3113e6679 (accessed March 12, 2022).

Perlis, M. 2013. "5 Characteristics Of Grit—How Many Do You Have?" www.forbes.com/sites/margaretperlis/2013/10/29/5-characteristics-of-grit-what-it-is-why-you-need-it-and-do-you-have-it/?sh=54700d6e4f7b (accessed May 21, 2021).

Plowman, D., L. Baker, T. Beck, M. Kulkarni, S. Solansky, and D. Travis. 2007. "Radical Change Accidently; The Emergence and Amplification of Small Change." *Academy of Management* 50, no. 3.

Poscente, V. 2008. *The Age of Speed*. New York, NY: Ballantine.

Proctor, A. 2020. "Why Increasing Organizational Resilience to Change Matters." https://blog.changefirst.com/blog/2014/08/increase-your-resilience-to-change (accessed April 02, 2021).

Pulakos, E., and R.B. Kaiser. April 07, 2020. "To Build an Agile Team, Commit to Organizational Stability." *Harvard Business Review*. https://hbr.org/2020/04/to-build-an-agile-team-commit-to-organizational-stability

Puusa, A., and U. Toivanen. 2006. "Organizational Identity and Trust." *Electronic Journal of Business Ethics and Organization Studies* 11, no. 2.

Quattrone, P., and T. Hopper. 2001. "What Does Organizational Change Mean?" *Management Accounting Research* 12, no. 4, pp. 403–435.

Quay Consulting. n.d. *Embedding Organizational Change Management for Success*. www.quayconsulting.com.au/news/embedding-organisational-change-management-for-success/ (accessed April 06, 2021).

Reeves, M., and M. Deimler. May 27, 2011. "Adaptability: The New Competitive Advantage." *Harvard Business Review*. https://hbr.org/2011/07/adaptability-the-new-competitive-advantage

Reilly, A., J. Brett, and L. Stroh. 1993. "The Impact of Corporate Turbulence on Manager's Attitudes." *Strategic Management Journal* 14, pp. 167–179.

Rosenberg, S., and J. Mosca. 2011. "Breaking Down the Barriers to Organizational Change." *International Journal of Management & Information Systems* 15, no. 3.

Sattar, S.B. July 30, 2020. "Leadership Qualities, Skills, and Style of Jeff Bezos." The Strategy Watch. www.thestrategywatch.com/leadership-qualities-skills-style-jeff-bezos/

Schneeweiss, C. 2012. *Distributed Decision Making*, 2nd ed. Springer

Schultz, J.S., E. Sjøvold, and B. André. 2017. "Can Formal Innovation Training Improve Group- and Organizational-Level Innovativeness in a Healthcare Setting?" *Journal of Innovation and Entrepreneurship* 6, no. 1. *& Organization Development Journal* 25, no. 3/4, pp. 332–345.

SeedAdvisory. n.d. *The VUCA World*. www.seedhk.com/vuca/ (accessed February 07, 2021).

Siebert, A. 2005. *The Resiliency Advantage: Master Change, Thrive Under Pressure and Bounce Back from Setbacks*. San Francisco: Berrett-Koehler Publishers, Inc.

Segal, E. 2021. *Leaders And Employees Are Burning Out At Record Rates: New Survey*. www.forbes.com/sites/edwardsegal/2021/02/17/leaders-and-employees-are-burning-out-at-record-rates-new-survey/?sh=4e3c59d36499 (accessed April 13, 2021).

Senge, P., A. Kleiner, C. Roberts, R. Ross, G. Roth, and B. Smith. 1999. *The Dance of Change*. New York, NY: Doubleday.

Senior, B., and S. Swailes. 2009. *Organizational Change*. New York, NY: Pearson.

Shepardson, D. March 22, 2021. "Exclusive: U.S. Senators Press Biden to Set End Date for Gas-Powered Car Sales." U.S. www.reuters.com/article/us-autos-emissions-california-exclusive-idUSKBN2BE111

Sibbet, D., and G. Wendling. 2018. *Visual Consulting: Designing & Leading Change*. Hoboken, N.J: John Wiley & Sons.

Sikora, P., E. Beaty, and J. Forward. 2004. "Updating Theory on Organizational Stress: The Asynchronous Multiple Overlapping Change (AMOC) Model of Workplace Stress." *Human Resource Development Review* 3, no. 1, pp. 3–35.

Sinek, S. 2019. *The Infinite Game*. New York, NY: Portfolio/Penquin.

Smarp. 2021. *What is Change Communication and How to Get it Right*. Available at March 14, 2021 from https://blog.smarp.com/change-communication-definition-and-best-practices

Smith, C. 2015. "Creating Organizational Readiness for Change." https://change.walkme.com/creating-organizational-readiness-for-change/ (accessed April 02, 2021).

Smith, C. 2019. "The ADKAR Model of Change Management: Pros and Cons." https://change.walkme.com/adkar-model/ (accessed March 31, 2021).

Smith, S. 1997. "The Satir Change Model." https://stevenmsmith.com/ar-satir-change-model/ (accessed March 31, 2021).

Spector, P. 2019. "What is Organizational Climate?" http://paulspector.com/organizational-behavior/what-is-organizational-climate/ (accessed April 04, 2021).

Spillane, J.P. 2012. *Distributed Leadership.* Wiley.

Stiehm, J., and N. Townsend. 2002. *The U.A. Army War College: Military Education in a Democracy.* Philadelphia, PA: Temple University Press.

Tams, C. 2018. "Why We Need To Rethink Organizational Change Management." www.forbes.com/sites/carstentams/2018/01/26/why-we-need-to-rethink-organizational-change-management/?sh=3f5d97d0e93c (accessed April 30, 2021).

Thompson, D. December 14, 2020. "The Workforce Is About to Change Dramatically." *The Atlantic.* www.theatlantic.com/ideas/archive/2020/08/just-small-shift-remote-work-could-change-everything/614980/

Tiong, T. 2005. "Maximizing Human Resource Potential in the Midst of Organizational Change." *Singapore Management Review* 27, no. 2, pp. 25–36.

Torres, R., and N. Rimmer. December 21, 2011. "The Five Traits of Highly Adaptive Leadership Teams." *BCG Global.* www.bcg.com/publications/2011/people-organization-five-traits-highly-adaptive-leadership-teams

Trompenaars, F., and P. Woolliams. 2003. "A New Framework for Managing Change Across Cultures." *Journal of Change Management* 3, no. 4, pp. 361–375.

Uhl-Bien, M., and M. Arena. 2018. "Leadership for Organizational Adaptability: A Theoretical Synthesis and Integrative Framework." *The Leadership Quarterly* 29, no. 1, pp. 89–104

Uotila, J. 2017. "Exploration, Exploitation and Variability: Competition for Primacy Revisited." *Strategic Organization* 15, no. 4, pp. 461–480.

Valdellon, L. 2017. "11 Key Business Benefits of Team Collaboration (& Why You Should Work on Your Teamwork)." www.wrike.com/blog/business-benefits-of-team-collaboration/ (accessed April 01, 2021).

Van Dick, R., U. Wagner, and G. Lemmer. 2004. "Research Note: The Winds of Change–Multiple Identifications in the Case of Organizational Mergers." *European Journal of Work and Organizational Psychology* 13, no. 2, pp. 121–138.

Venkatraman, V.N. June 24, 2019. "Netflix: A Case of Transformation for the Digital Future." *Medium,* https://medium.com/@nvenkatraman/netflix-a-case-of-transformation-for-the-digital-future-4ef612c8d8b

Völpel, S. 2003. *The Mobile Company, An Advanced Organizational Model for Mobilizing Knowledge Innovation and Value Creation.* IFPM: St. Gallen.

Wanberg, C., and J. Banas. 2000. "Predictors and Outcomes of Openness to Changes in a Reorganizing Workplace." *Journal of Applied Psychology* 85, no. 1, pp. 132–142.

Waterson, P., C. Clegg, W. Bolden, K. Pepper, P. Warr, and T. Wall. 1999. "The Use and Effectiveness of Modern Manufacturing Practices: A Survey of UK Industry." *International Journal of Production Research* 37, pp. 2271–2292.

Weiner, B., H. Amick, and S. Lee. 2008. "Review: Conceptualization and Measurement of Organizational Readiness for Change." *Medical Care Research and Review* 65, no. 4, pp. 379–436.

Westover, J. 2020. "The Role of Systems Thinking in Organizational Change and Development." www.forbes.com/sites/forbescoachescouncil/2020/06/15/the-role-of-systems-thinking-in-organizational-change-and-development/?sh=3fe93d622c99 (accessed May 01, 2021).

Wischnevsky, D. 2004. "Change as the Winds Change: The Impact of Organizational Transformation on Firm Survival in a Shifting Environment." *Organizational Analysis* 12, no. 4, pp. 361–377.

Y Scouts. 2018. "Six Drivers of Change for the Future Workforce." https://yscouts.com/blog/six-drivers-of-change-for-the-future-workforce/ (accessed May 28, 2021).

Yoon, C. August 31, 2018. "Assumptions that Led to the Failure of Google Glass." *Medium.* medium.com/nyc-design/the-assumptions-that-led-to-failures-of-google-glass-8b40a

Youngman, R. 2020. "Farewell and Good Riddance." www.cleantech.com/farewell-and-good-riddance-2020-your-chaotic-legacy-will-live-on-for-good-or-for-bad/ (accessed February 06, 2021).

Zhang, H. 2014. "GE Change Management (CAP)." www.slideshare.net/HomerZhang/ge-change-managementcap (accessed March 31, 2021).

About the Authors

Dr. Richard Dool is currently the Managing Director of Leaderocity™, LLC. He developed this consulting practice to focus in these primary areas: leadership communication, change management, strategic development, and organizational renewal.

Dr. Dool has a comprehensive and diverse executive level leadership background including leading an $800 million division of AT&T, global commercial leadership roles at GE, and serving for 12 years as CEO of both public and private companies. His background includes rescuing a company from near bankruptcy, leading the acquisition or divestiture of 11 companies, and effectively managing companies in the United States, UK, China, Brazil, Germany, France, India, and Australia. He has a significant operational history in general management, sales/commercial leadership, product management, and marketing leadership positions. He comes with a successful leadership experience in a variety of settings including multinational, multicultural, and virtual environments. He has been on the board of directors of five different companies as well as a member of several boards of advisors.

After his corporate career, Dr. Dool decided to pivot and pay it forward in academia. Dr. Dool is on the faculty at Rutgers University where he is also the Director of the Masters in Communication and Media and the Masters in Health Communication and Information programs.

Dr. Dool has a MA in strategic communication and leadership, a MS in management, and a doctorate in management/organizational processes. Dr. Dool is an active researcher and presenter in these areas and has published on the concepts of Change Fatigue™ and Leaderocity™. He is the author of *Enervative Change: The Impact of Persistent Change Initiatives on Job Satisfaction*, *12 Months of Leadership Insights*, *Leading in Difficult Times and Circumstances*, and *Leaderocity™: Leading at the Speed of Now*.

www.linkedin.com/in/richard-dool

Tahsin I. Alam is Associate Dean of Advancement for the Foster School of Business at the University of Washington (UW) in Seattle. He serves as a member of the Foster Advisor Board and is part of the dean's senior leadership team and University Advancement's Executive Leadership Team.

A higher education advancement industry veteran with over 17 years of experience in presidential and advancement professional searches, Mr. Alam began his career as an associate with Isaacson Miller, a Boston-based national search firm. After eight years of working with the development and alumni relations search practice, Mr. Alam went on to become a managing associate with the Nonprofit Professional Advisory Group (NPAG), a boutique consulting firm with clients across the nonprofit sector. Here he served as a partner for the development and communications search practice, where in four years, the practice grew from inception to the most profitable practice at the firm.

At the Rutgers University Foundation, Tahsin served as the Vice President for Advancement Services and Talent Management. He oversaw 70 employees across the departments of talent management, donor relations, stewardship, prospect research, prospect management, board relations, and campaign operations. Outside of Rutgers, Mr. Alam is a consulting partner with BWF, one of the leading consulting firms in the advancement industry. Mr. Alam holds a bachelor of arts degree in politics, economics, and theater from Bates College and a master's in organizational communications from Rutgers University. He is a native of Bangladesh.

www.linkedin.com/in/tahsin-alam/

Index

OTHER TITLES IN THE HUMAN RESOURCE MANAGEMENT AND ORGANIZATIONAL BEHAVIOR COLLECTION

Michael Provitera, Barry University, Editor

- *Versatility in the Age of Specialization* by Angela Cotellessa
- *Championing the Cause of Leadership* by Ted Meyer
- *Embracing Ambiguity* by Michael Edmondson
- *Breaking the Proactive Paradox* by Tim Baker
- *The Modern Trusted Advisor* by MacKay Nancy and Weiss Alan
- *Achieving Success as a 21st Century Manager* by Dean E. Frost
- *A.I. and Remote Working* by Miller Tony
- *Best Boss!* by Ferguson Duncan, Toni M. Pristo, and John Furcon
- *Managing for Accountability* by Curry Lynne
- *Fundamentals of Level Three Leadership* by Clawson James G.S.
- *Emotional Connection: The EmC Strategy* by Gershfeld Lola and Sedehi Ramin
- *Civility at Work* by Bayer Lewena
- *Lean on Civility* by Masotti Christian and Bayer Lewena
- *Agility* by Edmondson Michael
- *Strengths Oriented Leadership* by Beadle Matt

Concise and Applied Business Books

The Collection listed above is one of 30 business subject collections that Business Expert Press has grown to make BEP a premiere publisher of print and digital books. Our concise and applied books are for...

- Professionals and Practitioners
- Faculty who adopt our books for courses
- Librarians who know that BEP's Digital Libraries are a unique way to offer students ebooks to download, not restricted with any digital rights management
- Executive Training Course Leaders
- Business Seminar Organizers

Business Expert Press books are for anyone who needs to dig deeper on business ideas, goals, and solutions to everyday problems. Whether one print book, one ebook, or buying a digital library of 110 ebooks, we remain the affordable and smart way to be business smart. For more information, please visit www.businessexpertpress.com, or contact sales@businessexpertpress.com.